A GLASS OF WATER

"Verre d'eau"

Smith and Kraus *Books For Actors*

THE MONOLOGUE SERIES

The Best Men's / Women's Stage Monologues of 1994
The Best Men's / Women's Stage Monologues of 1993
The Best Men's / Women's Stage Monologues of 1992
The Best Men's / Women's Stage Monologues of 1991
The Best Men's / Women's Stage Monologues of 1990
One Hundred Men's / Women's Stage Monologues from the 1980's
2 Minutes and Under: Original Character Monologues for Actors
Street Talk: Original Character Monologues for Actors
Uptown: Original Character Monologues for Actors
Ice Babies in Oz: Original Character Monologues for Actors
Monologues from Contemporary Literature: Volume I
Monologues from Classic Plays
100 Great Monologues from the Renaissance Theatre
100 Great Monologues from the Neo-Classical Theatre
100 Great Monologues from the 19th C. Romantic and Realistic Theatres

CONTEMPORARY PLAYWRIGHTS SERIES

Romulus Linney: 17 Short Plays
Eric Overmyer: Collected Plays
Lanford Wilson: 21 Short Plays
William Mastrosimone: Collected Plays
Horton Foote: 4 New Plays
Israel Horovitz Vol. I: 16 Short Plays
Terrence McNally: 15 Short Plays
Humana Festival '93: The Complete Plays
Humana Festival '94: The Complete Plays
Humana Festival '95: The Complete Plays
Women Playwrights: The Best Plays of 1992
Women Playwrights: The Best Plays of 1993
Women Playwrights: The Best Plays of 1994
EST Marathon '94: One-Act Plays
EST Marathon '95: One-Act Plays
Showtime's Act One Festival '95: One-Act Plays
By the Sea, By the Sea, By the Beautiful Sea: *McNally, Pintauro, Wilson*

GREAT TRANSLATION FOR ACTORS SERIES

Mercadet by Honoré de Balzac, tr. by Robert Cornthwaite
Zoyka's Apartment by Mikhail Bulgakov, tr. by N. Saunders & F. Dwyer
The Wood Demon by Anton Chekhov, tr. by N. Saunders & F. Dwyer
The Sea Gull by Anton Chekhov, tr. by N. Saunders & F. Dwyer
Three Sisters by Anton Chekhov, tr. by Lanford Wilson
The Coffee Shop by Carlo Goldoni, tr. by Robert Cornthwaite
Villeggiatura: The Trilogy by Carlo Goldoni, tr. by Robert Cornthwaite
Summer People by Maxim Gorky, tr. by N. Saunders & F. Dwyer
Ibsen: 4 Major Plays, tr. by Rick Davis & Brian Johnston
Spite for Spite by Agustín Moreto, tr. by Dakin Matthews
Cyrano de Bergerac by Edmond Rostand, tr. by Charles Marowitz

CAREER DEVELOPMENT SERIES

The Job Book: 100 Acting Jobs for Actors
The Smith and Kraus Monologue Index
What to Give Your Agent for Christmas and 100 Other Tips for the Working Actor
The Camera Smart Actor
The Sanford Meisner Approach
Anne Bogart: Viewpoints
The Actor's Chekhov
Kiss and Tell: Restoration Scenes, Monologues, & History
Cold Readings: Some Do's and Don'ts for Actors at Auditions

If you require pre-publication information about upcoming Smith and Kraus books, you may receive our semi-annual catalogue, free of charge, by sending your name and address to *Smith and Kraus Catalogue, P.O. Box 127, One Main Street, Lyme, NH 03768. Or call us at (800) 895-4331, fax (603) 795-4427.*

A GLASS OF WATER
by Eugène Scribe

translated by Robert Cornthwaite

Great Translations for Actors Series

SK
A Smith and Kraus Book

HUMCA

A Smith and Kraus Book
Published by Smith and Kraus, Inc.

Manufactured in the United States of America
Cover and Text Design by Julia Hill
Cover art: Claude Monet, *The Houses of Parlament, Sunset,*
Chester Dale Collection, ©1995 Board of Trustees, National Gallery of Art, Washington

First Edition: December 1995
10 9 8 7 6 5 4 3 2 1

Library of Congress Cataloguing-in-Publication Data

Scribe, Eugène, 1791-1861.
[Verre d'eau. English]
A glass of water / by Eugène Scribe : translated by Robert Cornthwaite. --1st ed.
p. cm. --(Great translations for actors series)
"A Smith and Kraus Book."
ISBN 1-57525-003-9
I. Cornthwaite, Robert, 1917– . II. Title. III. Series.
PQ2425.V513 1995
842'.7--dc20 95-32905
CIP

Contents

Foreword

Le théâtre a payé cet asyle champêtre:
Vous qui passez, merci! Je vous le dois peut-être.
(The theater paid for this sanctum, and so
To the passerby, thanks! It is you I may owe.)
—*Inscription over the entrance*
to Scribe's magnificent country house

Augustin Eugène Scribe (1791-1861), son of a silk merchant, was that rare bird, a writer who wrung fame, popularity and fabulous fortune out of his writing while revolutionizing French drama and opera with liberal political and religious ideas. Scribe flooded the stage with dramas, comedies, farces—some four hundred nineteen of them by one count—reflecting the society of his day in its serious as well as its comic aspects. He and Balzac were among the first to mirror bourgeois morality and life; but Scribe achieved something Balzac, Zola, and even Molière never did in their lifetimes: He was elected to the French Academy.

Like Balzac's *Mercadet* (1840), Scribe's *Glass of Water,* (*Le verre d'eau*) also from 1840, shows how fascinated the French were at the beginning of the Victorian age by all things English.

A Glass of Water takes up the story of Queen Anne and the Marlboroughs in 1710, when the famous duke was generalissimo of the armies allied against Louis XIV. The Duke of Marlborough was the ogre of whom French children sang "Malbrouk(*sic*)s'en va-t-en guerre" in mockery. They still do.

But the duke is offstage throughout Scribe's fast-moving comedy. It is his duchess who precipitates the action in her determination to dominate the queen and snatch a handsome young guardsman from her and from Abigail Churchill, a cousin of the Marlboroughs.

Churchill was the duke's family name—a name made even more famous by a modern descendant of the Marlboroughs, the historian and politician who led Britain through the Second World War—Winston Churchill. Between 1933 and 1938 this latter-day Churchill published a four-volume biography of his eighteenth-century ancestor and then went on himself to become perhaps the best known of all "king's first ministers."

Of course Scribe re-arranges history to suit his purpose. All good dramatists from the Greeks onward have done the same in order to insure a well-constructed play. Shakespeare, for instance, certainly did his share of shifting facts around in his chronicle or history plays. He took his plots from Holinshed and Plutarch, as they had taken their sources wherever they could find them, frequently from any juicy gossip floating around. History is a long piece of embroidery in which the stitches are put in by many hands and in many colors.

So, in *A Glass of Water* the real or historical Abigail Hill, a relative of the Tory politician Robert Harley, is transformed into "Abigail Churchill," a cousin of the ducal Marlboroughs, which she was—or rather they were, the real and the theatrical Abigails. The man she married, Samuel Masham, willy-nilly has his name changed by Scribe to "Arthur." Arthur does have a nice legendary ring to it, and perhaps Samuel sounded too Semitic to a nineteenth-century Frenchman. After all Samuel was a Hebrew of the Old Testament.

Queen Anne actually was a forty-five-year-old widow who had borne seventeen children by 1710, the time of this play. Never mind; in *A Glass of Water* she becomes a virgin smitten by first love.

Still, Scribe sticks to many facts that can be verified. The young Abigail did become "bedchamber woman to the queen" in life as on stage; and she did replace Sarah Churchill, the Duchess of Marlborough, "mistress of the robes," as Queen Anne's favorite and the power behind the throne.

Lord Henry St. John, later Viscount Bolingbrʲke, did write for the *Examiner* and repeatedly served as cabinet minister.

As for the Marquis de Torcy, he was indeed Louis XIV's representative at the peace negotiations; but he did not come to the court of England at the time of the events portrayed.

On the question of Masham's sex appeal and how overpowering it may have been, the issue remains a matter of conjecture. "Arthur" in the play probably outsizzles the real Samuel. Why shouldn't he? Stage lighting and a costume with the proper padding can do wonders. Improper padding might do even more.

　　　　　　　&a.　　&a.　　&a.

While Scribe's goal, quite like Shakespeare's, was success at the box-office, he also achieved a kind of classic status—the classic of the well-made play. He was no poet like Shakespeare but a master craftsman, the greatest improviser of the age. "The rules of the well-made play are the rules of the theater because they are the rules of logic," says Sarcey in *Quarante ans de théâtre*, Vol. VII, p. 227.

One rule was that there must be plenty of action. Action to Scribe was more important than psychology or character study or atmosphere. A good play must have ingenious *coups de théâtre* and surprises.

So Scribe piles up the surprises in *A Glass of Water*. Masham explains in the first scene why Bolingbroke must not expect Abigail to appear:

MASHAM: Coming to the royal palace frightens her.
BOLINGBROKE: She'll come. The thought of joining you here will fetch her.
　　(Enter Abigail.)
　　What did I tell you? Here she is.

　　　　　　　　　　&a

BOLINGBROKE: That note...was written by your new patroness herself (and you don't know who she is)?

ABIGAIL: Yes…Do you know the handwriting?
BOLINGBROKE: (*coolly*) Yes, my child, I do. It's the queen's.

ε

ABIGAIL: (*seeing the door open*) Arthur's coming back.
BOLINGBROKE: No. Better yet—it's our proud duchess.

ε

The Duchess of Marlborough catches sight of Abigail and says:

DUCHESS: This little jeweler's girl is the person the queen spoke of (as a candidate to be lady-in-waiting)? Service to the queen requires a distinguished family.
BOLINGBROKE: Hers is dazzling.
DUCHESS: Really? So many claim noble birth.
BOLINGBROKE: That's why this young lady hesitates to tell you that her name is Abigail Churchill.
DUCHESS: (*whose name is Sarah Churchill*) Oh hell!

ε

ABIGAIL: Everything goes wrong…except for my Arthur.
    (*Arthur Masham, looking distraught, runs in.*)
MASHAM: Oh thank heaven, here you are! I was looking for you!
ABIGAIL: Arthur! What's the matter?
MASHAM: I'm in a terrible fix! (I killed a man!)

ε

All these "surprises" occur in the first fifteen pages. There are many more to come:

DUCHESS: So it's agreed—you'll not see little Abigail again?
QUEEN: Agreed.
    (*Thompson comes in to announce:*)

THOMPSON: Miss Abigail Churchill.
DUCHESS: Oh hell!

ᘒ

Masham flees the court to save his life after the killing, and Abigail prays for his safe escape:

ABIGAIL: Dear Lord, I ask nothing for myself, but let Arthur
    reach the continent safely. Let him live… He left yesterday
    so he should be far away by now…Aaaa!
    (She cries out as Arthur Masham enters.)
    What brings you back to London?
MASHAM: *(calmly)* I never left.

ᘒ

QUEEN: *(to Abigail with quiet urgency)* That person we talked
    about…? I must see him.
ABIGAIL: *(Lightly, not knowing it is Masham the queen loves)* Who?
    The dream hero?
QUEEN: Yes. Bring him to me.
ABIGAIL: For that, I'd have to know who he is.
    *(The queen turns and sees Masham, who has just entered with
    the queen's gloves and Bible.)*
QUEEN: Here he is now.
ABIGAIL: *(immobile with surprise)* Oh my God!

ᘒ

Bolingbroke and the Duchess of Marlborough have reached a stalemate in their eternal feuding:

BOLINGBROKE: I pledge truce for today, frank and open.
DUCHESS: So be it!
    (She extends her hand and Bolingbroke raises it to his lips.)

DUCHESS: And tomorrow—war!
  Curtain.

❧

MEMBER OF PARLIAMENT: The *marquis* must leave the country
  tomorrow, without once seeing the queen.
THOMPSON: *(announcing)* His Excellency the Ambassador of
  France, the Marquis de Torcy!
  (The surprise is general.)

❧

ABIGAIL: Masham is under guard. Lord Henry would never set
  him free. It's impossible.
  (Masham enters.)
QUEEN: Hush! Here he is!
ABIGAIL: Oh heavens!

❧

These examples illustrate another basic rule. In farce, which is
the well-made play taken to its extreme as in the intricate precision-
tooled work of Feydeau later in the century, the rule is: The next person through the door must be the person least expected.

❧ ❧ ❧

The theme of *A Glass of Water* is spoken by Lord Henry St. John: "Little things can lead to great ones. This war with France sprang from the wounded vanity of a courtesan. And look at me! Do you know how Henry St. John—once considered a dandy and a blockhead—do you know how I became a cabinet minister? Because I knew the latest dance-step, the saraband. And do you know why I lost power? I caught a cold."

❧ ❧ ❧

Phyllis Hartnoll sums up Scribe's place in *A Concise History of the Theatre,* p. 183, Thames and Hudson, London 1968:

"The true theatre of the time was still to be found in vaudeville and melodrama, and in the works of the prolific Scribe, who during all the excesses of Romanticism continued imperturbably to turn out his 'well-made' plays, which set a pattern for dramatists everywhere. Unlike the Romantics, who made high tragedy of everyday happenings, Scribe excelled in bringing great historical events down to the level of the back parlour. His technique was superb. His closely-knit plots and orderly tying-off of loose ends appealed to the orderly French mind, and provided a welcome relief to an audience which had been introduced somewhat hurriedly to the splendid irrelevancies of Shakespeare and his imitators."

—Robert Cornthwaite

Cast

A Glass of Water

ACT I

Scene: Morning. A handsome reception hall. Door at the rear. Doors at either side. At left a desk, at right a table.

At Rise: Masham is asleep in an armchair near the door right. The Marquis de Torcy and Bolingbroke enter left.

BOLINGBROKE: I promise you, my lord *marquis*, I shall find some way to get this letter of yours to the queen…and it will be received with the respect due the envoy of Louis XIV.

DE TORCY: I count on that, Lord St. John. My sovereign still dreams of an honorable peace, and it will break this old man's heart if these negotiations bog down. My honor and that of France are in your hands.

BOLINGBROKE: I shall not fail you. People may tell you Henry St. John is an opinionated writer and a rabble–rousing politician—at least I hope they will!—but no one can say I ever betrayed a friend.

DE TORCY: I know that. I put all my hopes in you—my friend!

(He goes out. Bolingbroke is about to go out the other way when he passes Masham's chair and hears him talking in his sleep.)

MASHAM: Ah…! She's beautiful…

BOLINGBROKE: Youth! The time of illusions!

MASHAM: *(Still asleep.)* I love you…I'll always love you…

BOLINGBROKE: Only in your dreams, my boy. *(Recognizing the young officer.)* Well, Masham! I thought you looked familiar.

MASHAM: *(Dreaming.)* Such happiness…and such good fortune…it's too much, too much…

BOLINGBROKE: *(Tapping his shoulder.)* Then you'd better wake up.

MASHAM: *(Rousing.)* Hm? What is it? Oh…Lord St. John…

BOLINGBROKE: *(Laughing.)* I spoiled your dream of good fortune.

MASHAM: *(Rising.)* You? I'm still in your debt.

BOLINGBROKE: For what?

MASHAM: Two hundred guineas you gave me to save my hide, remember?

BOLINGBROKE: Oh yes. Still, I'd change places with you any day. I owe a hundred times more than that.

MASHAM: Does it make you miserable too?

BOLINGBROKE: No—actually I never felt freer. At your age I had squandered my fortune and was bankrupt. So they married me to a charming lady who had a dowry of a million—and as many whims. She was impossible to live with, so I gave her back her dowry—and learned to work for the first time in my life. But in

my idle youth—and especially in my marriage—I thought a
dozen times of killing myself.

MASHAM: You too?

BOLINGBROKE: Especially when I had to take my wife dancing. But
now I haven't time enough for all I want to do. Mornings I speak
in the House of Commons, and at night I write for my newspaper. The Duke of Marlborough at the head of his armies trem-
bles at my speeches in Parliament or my articles in the *Examiner*.
Marlborough wants war; I want peace and the prosperity of England. My task is to make the queen understand that.

MASHAM: Not an easy job.

BOLINGBROKE: No. Cannons impress people. The queen, like many
others, can't believe a conquering general can be a fool and a thief;
but I shall show Marlborough slipping his hand into the treasury.

MASHAM: Oh, you can't say that!

BOLINGBROKE: I've written it; I've signed my name to it. The article
will appear today. Eventually one voice always makes itself heard,
louder than the trumpets and the drums—the voice of truth!—
Forgive me, I thought I was in Parliament. I'm haranguing you
like Whigs in the House of Commons when you have dreams of
your own—dreams of fortune and love.

MASHAM: Who told you that?

BOLINGBROKE: You did. You talk in your sleep.

MASHAM: What did I say?

BOLINGBROKE: You were moaning about your good fortune. What's
the great lady's name?

MASHAM: I know no great ladies. My good fortune must come from some friend of my father's… Could it be you?

BOLINGBROKE: No, believe me.

MASHAM: You are the only one I can imagine… You see, when I decided to seek a place in the household of the queen, I tried to reach her as she was on her way to open Parliament. I pushed through the crowds toward her carriage, but before I could present my petition, a gentleman I had jostled turned and struck me in the face with the back of his hand.

BOLINGBROKE: Oh no!

MASHAM: Oh yes! I can still see him sneering at me. If I ever meet him again…! I managed to hand the queen my petition, and two weeks later came a letter granting me an audience with Her Majesty. I dressed in my best and hurried to the palace. I had just reached here on foot, in sight of some ladies standing on the balcony, when a carriage passed and spattered me with mud from head to foot—my one and only brocaded satin! And in the window of the carriage I saw *him* laughing at me—the man who had slapped me! I rushed after him but the carriage disappeared…and of course I missed my audience with the queen.

BOLINGBROKE: And your fortune.

MASHAM: No! Next day a fine suit of court clothes arrived—and an appointment as attendant to the queen! And shortly after that— a commission as ensign in the Guards!

BOLINGBROKE: Really! And you have no idea who your benefactor may be?

MASHAM: None at all. He assures me his favor will continue if I prove worthy. The only restriction is that I'm not to marry.

Act I

BOLINGBROKE: Aha!

MASHAM: Because it would hinder my promotion in the Guards, I suppose.

BOLINGBROKE: That's all that strikes you about this restriction?

MASHAM: What else could it be?

BOLINGBROKE: For a young man who has been at court three months your innocence is almost biblical.

MASHAM: Why?

BOLINGBROKE: *(Smiling.)* Your unknown benefactor is a benefactress.

MASHAM: What an idea!

BOLINGBROKE: Some great lady is interested in you.

MASHAM: Oh no, my lord. No, that's not possible.

BOLINGBROKE: What's so astonishing? Queen Anne is very respectable and good, so the court is royally bored. The ladies here amuse themselves with handsome young officers who never see a battle-field and yet achieve remarkable military promotions. Their rapid rise is all the more impressive because it has nothing to do with soldiering.

MASHAM: Oh, if I had known…

BOLINGBROKE: Now if you were *ordered* to marry, it would be a different story. But you are forbidden, so obedience shouldn't be difficult.

MASHAM: *(Standing by Bolingbroke's chair.)* But if...if I love some-one...and someone loves me...

BOLINGBROKE: Oh, I see. The one you were dreaming about just now?

MASHAM: Yes, my lord. The sweetest girl in London.

BOLINGBROKE: Who is she?

MASHAM: An orphan like me, a shopgirl in the City for a jeweler, Mister Tomwood...

BOLINGBROKE: Good Lord!

MASHAM: ...but he is going out of business, so she has no work and no resources.

BOLINGBROKE: *(Rising.)* Little Abigail?

MASHAM: You know her?

BOLINGBROKE: Through my wife, while we were still together. My wife was a good customer of Tomwood's. She loved the shop and I liked the shopgirl. You're right, Masham—she's charming.

MASHAM: Were you in love with her?

BOLINGBROKE: For a week perhaps...until I realized I was wasting my time. Look, we might find a post for Abigail here at court...

MASHAM: ...as lady in waiting—that's what I told her! Perhaps to the old Countess of Westmorland. She is looking for someone to read to her.

BOLINGBROKE: Not a bad idea.

MASHAM: I urged Abigail to apply for the post this morning, but coming to the royal palace frightens her.

BOLINGBROKE: She'll come. The thought of joining you here will fetch her.

(Enter Abigail.)

What did I tell you? Here she is!

ABIGAIL: Lord St. John!

(She gives Masham her hand.)

BOLINGBROKE: You were born under a lucky star! Your first time at court you find two friends! That doesn't happen often!

ABIGAIL: I am lucky, especially today.

MASHAM: You mean the Countess of Westmorland…?

ABIGAIL: No. The post has been taken.

MASHAM: And you're happy about it?

ABIGAIL: I have another—a better one!

MASHAM: How did it happen?

ABIGAIL: By chance, pure chance. Can you imagine! At Tomwood's shop there was one especially gracious lady who always came to me to buy. And looking at diamonds we used to chat…

BOLINGBROKE: And Miss Abigail chats enchantingly.

ABIGAIL: I could see this lady was not happy, because she would often say with a sigh how fortunate I was. Me!—stuck behind the counter, never getting away to see Mister Masham except on Sundays! About a month ago this kind lady took a fancy to a little gold box we had on sale—exquisite workmanship, and almost nothing—thirty guineas! But she had forgotten her purse, so I said we'll send it to my lady's home. She seemed embarrassed to say where she lived—probably because she didn't want her husband to know; there are great ladies who don't tell their husbands, you see!—so I said, "Look, my lady, I'll stand good for it myself," and gave it to her. She said she'd be back. Well, I waited and waited…

BOLINGBROKE: *(Laughing.)* The great lady was a cheat.

ABIGAIL: I began to think so. A month went by, and Mister Tomwood was doing badly in his business; his creditors were crowding around; and I owed him the thirty guineas. I decided I'd have to sell everything I owned—even this best dress of mine that becomes me, people say.

BOLINGBROKE: Indeed it does!

MASHAM: It makes you look even prettier, if that's possible.

ABIGAIL: That's why it was so hard to decide! I had just made up my mind to sell everything…when yesterday a carriage drives up to the shop, a lady gets out, and it's my lady! Affairs had kept her away, she said…she wasn't free to come and go as she pleased…and she wanted to pay in person… As she talked she noticed I'd been crying, and I had to tell her all about my predicament. Well, when she heard I was going to apply this morning to the Countess of Westmorland, she said don't go…you'll be unhappy…besides the place is taken. But…! she had a position she could offer me and would I accept it. I threw myself in her arms and said take me and I'll stay with you through whatever happens. She told me to come to the palace this morning and ask for this lady. *(She takes out a note.)*

MASHAM: How odd…

BOLINGBROKE: That note—may I see it? *(Smiling as Abigail gives it to him.)* Aha! I should have guessed. This was written by your new patroness herself?

ABIGAIL: Yes, right in front of me. Do you know the handwriting?

BOLINGBROKE: *(Coolly.)* Yes, my child, I do. It's the queen's.

ABIGAIL: *(Joyfully.)* The queen! Is that possible?

MASHAM: The queen gives you her favor? Your fortune's made!

BOLINGBROKE: *(Coming between them.)* Wait, my friends, wait a bit. Don't rejoice too soon.

ABIGAIL: But she's the queen! A queen can do as she likes!

BOLINGBROKE: Not this one. She's terrified of a woman she calls her best friend—Sarah Churchill, the Duchess of Marlborough. The duchess is more of a general than her husband and more of a queen than her sovereign.

ABIGAIL: The queen is devoted to this duchess?

BOLINGBROKE: She detests her…and her "best friend" returns the sentiment.

ABIGAIL: Then why not get rid of her?

BOLINGBROKE: My dear, in England it's not the queen who rules, it's the majority—the Whigs, the party of Marlborough and his duchess. The duchess supervises the queen's household, and any appointment made without her consent is in for trouble.

ABIGAIL: If it depends on the duchess, don't worry. I may have a chance.

MASHAM: How do you mean?

ABIGAIL: I'm a relative of hers…by misalliance. My father was a Churchill who broke with his family when he married my mother.

MASHAM: Really…a relative of the duchess!

ABIGAIL: A distant one. I would never approach her because she refused to recognize my mother. But I'm asking nothing from the duchess. I owe this appointment to the goodness of the queen.

BOLINGBROKE: You don't know the duchess! Still, I may be able to help you. I've nothing to lose; she hates me already.

ABIGAIL: That's very good of you.

MASHAM: How can we ever repay you?

BOLINGBROKE: With your friendship. *(Taking their hands.)* Between us from now on—alliance, offensive and defensive! Agreed?

ABIGAIL: *(Smiling.)* A feeble alliance, I'm afraid.

BOLINGBROKE: Stronger perhaps than you think. Two fronts to fight on, two objectives: the appointment for Abigail…and a letter I'd like to put in the hands of the queen. I've been waiting for the chance. Now, if Abigail is among the ladies attending on Her Majesty, all my messages can get through in spite of the duchess.

Act I

MASHAM: Is that all? I can do that for you. Every morning at ten—a few minutes from now—I take Her Majesty *(Getting the newspaper from the table right.)* the *Gazette*, which she skims through while drinking her tea. Sometimes she asks me to read her the articles about fashion.

BOLINGBROKE: Wonderful! *(Slipping de Torcy's letter into the Gazette.)* We'll slip the *marquis'* letter among the farthingales and furbelows. *(Taking a newspaper from his pocket.)* And while we're at it…

ABIGAIL: What are you doing?

BOLINGBROKE: …a copy of the *Examiner* too. Her Majesty will see how we treat the Duke and Duchess of Marlborough in our newspaper. She may be shocked, but it will please her—and she has so little pleasure! It's ten o'clock. Go, Masham, go.

MASHAM: Count on me. *(He goes out by the door right.)*

BOLINGBROKE: You see? The triple alliance is already at work. Masham is our shield and buckler.

ABIGAIL: Yes…but I'm worth so little to you.

BOLINGBROKE: Little things can lead to great ones. This war with France sprang from the wounded vanity of a courtesan. And look at me! Do you know how Henry St. John—once considered a dandy and a blockhead—do you know how I became a cabinet minister?

ABIGAIL: No…

BOLINGBROKE: Because I knew the latest dance-step, the saraband. And do you know why I lost power? I caught a cold.

ABIGAIL: Really?

BOLINGBROKE: *(Looking toward the queen's rooms.)* So now I carry on the fight in the ranks of the loyal opposition.

ABIGAIL: What can you do there?

BOLINGBROKE: Wait and hope—for some caprice of fate, some accidental pebble that may overturn the chariot of the conqueror. The more trivial it seems, the more important it may be.

ABIGAIL: *(Seeing the door open.)* Arthur's coming back.

BOLINGBROKE: No. Better yet—it's our proud duchess.

(The Duchess of Marlborough comes in from the gallery.)

ABIGAIL: *(Low.)* That's the Duchess of Marlborough?

BOLINGBROKE: *(Quietly.)* Your cousin…in the flesh.

ABIGAIL: I've seen her at the shop. She's the lady who bought the diamond clips.

(The Duchess looks up from the newspaper she is reading.)

DUCHESS: Lord St. John…

BOLINGBROKE: I was just thinking of Your Grace.

DUCHESS: As you do all too often. You're forever attacking me in the press.

BOLINGBROKE: I have no other means of getting your attention.

DUCHESS: *(Brandishing the paper.)* I'll remember you for today's issue, I promise you that.

Act I

BOLINGBROKE: You condescended to read it?

DUCHESS: It was on the queen's breakfast table. I have just come from Her Majesty.

BOLINGBROKE: *(Shaken.)* Ah, that's where…

DUCHESS: Yes. The officer of the Guards had brought her the *Gazette.*

BOLINGBROKE: They don't publish me.

DUCHESS: I know; you're not in fashion. But between the leaves of the *Gazette* was a copy of your scurrilous newspaper…and a letter from the Marquis de Torcy.

BOLINGBROKE: Addressed to the queen.

DUCHESS: That's why I read it.

BOLINGBROKE: *(Indignant.)* Your Grace!

DUCHESS: It's my duty. I read all letters to Her Majesty. So when you write some vicious attack on me, you must address it to the queen. That's the only way you can get me to read it.

BOLINGBROKE: I shall remember, Your Grace. But now Her Majesty is at least aware of the *marquis'* proposals, and that was my aim.

DUCHESS: You're mistaken. I read them first—and put them in the fire.

BOLINGBROKE: Really, Your Grace!

(The Duchess bows and starts out. She sees Abigail at the rear.)

DUCHESS: Who is that pretty child? What's her name?

(Abigail comes forward and curtsies.)

ABIGAIL: Abigail.

DUCHESS: Ah, the jeweler's girl. I recognize her. She's really not bad, this little one. And she's the person the queen spoke of?

ABIGAIL: *(Eagerly.)* Her Majesty told you about me?

DUCHESS: And left it to me to consent or refuse. I shall be impartial.

BOLINGBROKE: Then we're lost.

DUCHESS: You understand, young lady, there are qualifications.

BOLINGBROKE: *(Advancing.)* She has them, Lady Churchill.

DUCHESS: *(Alertly.)* Ah! You take an interest in this young person, my lord?

BOLINGBROKE: From the way you treated her, I thought you knew.

DUCHESS: Service to the queen requires a distinguished family.

BOLINGBROKE: Hers is dazzling.

DUCHESS: Really? So many claim noble birth.

BOLINGBROKE: That's why this young lady hesitates to tell you her name is Abigail Churchill.

DUCHESS: Oh hell!

BOLINGBROKE: A very distant relative, no doubt—but still a cousin of the Duchess of Marlborough. Your Grace will understand that for an old used–up writer like me there might be something in this

Act I

story. The readers of the *Examiner* would enjoy hearing about the noble duchess and her cousin the shopgirl. However, on condition that Abigail is appointed to Her Majesty's household...by you...today...I take an oath never to have heard of this story, piquant as it may be...

DUCHESS: *(Proudly.)* Whether or not she's my relative will not affect my decision. As for you, my lord, a journalist—and especially an opposition journalist—before he meddles in State affairs, should put his own affairs in order. You have enormous debts, which your creditors have sold me at fifteen percent on the pound. I've bought them all. *(Smiling.)* These debts of yours could lead to your imprisonment, something I have never done to a member of the House of Commons—at least not yet. Now, if the piquant story you mention should appear in your paper tomorrow morning, the evening journal will announce that its brilliant author is at that moment in Newgate prison. But I am sure you will see the wisdom of keeping quiet. *(She makes a reverence and leaves.)*

ABIGAIL: Well! What do you say to that?

BOLINGBROKE: *(Blithely.)* The duchess has done what my best friends wouldn't do—put out money for me. She must really hate me. Very flattering.

ABIGAIL: I don't want to go through with this. Your freedom is at stake.

BOLINGBROKE: We shall see! *(Looking at the clock on the wall.)* Oh good God! It's time for Commons to convene. I'm to speak against the Duke of Marlborough, who is demanding subsidies. I'll not vote him a shilling. Goodbye! Remember our alliance. *(He goes out left.)*

ABIGAIL: *(About to leave.)* A fine alliance, where everything goes wrong ...except for my Arthur.

(Masham, looking distraught, runs in from the rear.)

MASHAM: Oh thank heaven, here you are! I was looking for you.

ABIGAIL: Arthur! What's the matter?

MASHAM: I'm in a terrible fix!

ABIGAIL: So is Lord St. John!

MASHAM: In St. James Park, on one of the paths, I suddenly ran into him!

ABIGAIL: Who?

MASHAM: Him! The man who slapped me! I know he recognized me because he took one look at me and laughed. *(Enraged.)* He laughed at me again! I drew my sword...and he drew his... and...and...then he stopped laughing.

ABIGAIL: He's—dead?

MASHAM: I don't know. He staggered and... Then I heard people coming and I remembered the law against dueling.

ABIGAIL: On pain of death! You must leave London.

MASHAM: I will tomorrow.

ABIGAIL: Now!

MASHAM: What about you? And Lord St. John?

ABIGAIL: He's about to be arrested for debt, and I'll not get my appointment...but that doesn't matter. It's you! You're more important. You must get away!

Act I

MASHAM: Yes, but first I wanted to see you…embrace you…

ABIGAIL: Then hurry!

MASHAM: *(In her arms.)* Ah…!

ABIGAIL: *(Disengaging herself.)* Goodbye! Goodbye! If you love me, run! Run!

(They separate and run off in opposite directions.)

END OF ACT ONE

ACT II

Scene: The same. Morning.

At Rise: Queen Anne and Thompson.

QUEEN: You say they are from the House of Commons, Thompson?

THOMPSON: Yes, ma'am. They request an audience with Your Majesty.

QUEEN: More petitions! When I'm all alone! The duchess is away at Windsor! Did you tell them I don't see anyone…

THOMPSON: …before two o'clock, yes, ma'am. They gave me this paper. They'll come back at two and present their petitions to Your Majesty.

QUEEN: *(Putting the paper on the desk.)* The duchess will be here by that time. She can deal with them. Who were these people?

THOMPSON: Sir Robert Harley and Lord St. John.

QUEEN: Oh! Have they gone?

THOMPSON: Yes, ma'am.

QUEEN: I'm sorry to have missed Lord St. John. When he was in power everything went beautifully and I was never bored. With the duchess away, he and I could have had a chat.

THOMPSON: The duchess gave me a standing order—every time Lord St. John calls…

QUEEN: Oh…the duchess… That's different. And Lord St. John left no word?

THOMPSON: He wrote out the note I just gave Your Majesty.

QUEEN: *(Taking up the note.)* Good. You may go now.

(Thompson bows and leaves. She reads:)

"Madam, I came to beg an audience with Your Majesty and to bask in the sight of my sovereign, which has been denied me for so long." Poor Lord Henry! "That the duchess should keep her political opponents as far from you as possible is something I can understand; but her mistrust goes to the extreme of driving away a poor girl whose kindness and concern have lightened the cares which weigh upon Your Majesty. This girl is denied the place you wish to give her on the pretext that she is without noble family; and I wish to advise you myself that Abigail Churchill is cousin to the Duchess of Marlborough." Is it possible? "Will Your Majesty be good enough to keep the secret of your faithful servant, Henry St. John."

(She rings and Thompson appears.)

Thompson, go to Tomwood the jeweler's. Ask for Miss Abigail Churchill and tell her to come at once to the palace. I wish it. I order it, I—the queen! Now go.

THOMPSON: Yes, ma'am.

(He is about to leave as she continues:)

QUEEN: The duchess is beginning to weary me…

(Thompson, at the door, ushers in the Duchess, and then he goes. The Queen sits and conceals Bolingbroke's note in her bosom. The Duchess sees this and approaches the Queen, who turns her back.)

DUCHESS: May I presume to inquire of Her Majesty…what news?

QUEEN: *(Crossly.)* I am indisposed.

DUCHESS: Her Majesty is upset? Over my absence perhaps…

QUEEN: Yes. I don't see why you had to go to Windsor this morning and leave me here buried in work—petitions and appeals…

DUCHESS: Have you heard what is happening?

QUEEN: What?

DUCHESS: A very grave affair…very vexing. And dangerous.

QUEEN: Heavens!

DUCHESS: There are riots in the city. I shouldn't be surprised if there was a national uprising.

QUEEN: An uprising!

DUCHESS: We have stationed a regiment of dragoons in Windsor to march on London at a moment's notice. I have just conferred with the Chiefs of Staff, all devoted to my husband and Your Majesty.

QUEEN: Ah, that's why you went to Windsor.

DUCHESS: Yes, ma'am. And you were blaming me.

QUEEN: I was, duchess?

DUCHESS: *(Smiling.)* Well, you were very cool. I could see I was in disfavor.

QUEEN: Don't be angry, duchess. I'm in such a state…

DUCHESS: I can guess why. Your Majesty has received some bad news…

QUEEN: No…really…

DUCHESS: …which you do not wish to share for fear of wounding me or worrying me. I know Your Majesty's goodness.

QUEEN: You are mistaken.

DUCHESS: I saw it. When I came in you concealed a paper so hastily that it was easy to guess it concerned me.

QUEEN: No, duchess, I swear! It concerns only a young girl *(Taking the letter from her bosom.)* who is recommended to me by this letter— a young girl whom I wish…whom I intend to have a place among my ladies.

DUCHESS: *(Smiling and reaching for the letter.)* Really! If Your Majesty will permit…

QUEEN: *(Crumpling the letter.)* There's no need. It's little Abigail.

DUCHESS: Oh? And who is the person who recommended her so highly?

QUEEN: I promised not to reveal his name.

DUCHESS: From that alone I can deduce it's Lord St. John.

QUEEN: *(Anxiously.)* I didn't tell though, did I?

DUCHESS: *(Briskly.)* No, you didn't tell, ma'am, but I know he's the one.

QUEEN: What if he is?

DUCHESS: *(Curbing her anger.)* I see our enemies are winning. Our queen surrenders us into their hands at the very moment we are battling for her. Yes, ma'am, this very day a bill was introduced in Parliament to recall your brother Prince James to England and make him your heir. That bill caused these riots today. We support our queen against Henry St. John and his party at the risk of our political lives, while our queen, far from helping us, carries on a secret correspondence with our adversaries.

QUEEN: There's nothing political in this letter. It's simply...

DUCHESS: ...that Your Majesty is afraid to show it to me.

QUEEN: *(Impatiently.)* Out of regard for your feelings. *(Giving her the letter.)* It contains facts you cannot deny.

DUCHESS: *(Scanning the letter.)* Is that all? This is hardly earth-shattering.

QUEEN: It's true—you did oppose Abigail. And isn't she your cousin?

DUCHESS: Oh yes. That's why I didn't want her anywhere near Your Majesty. I have been accused of using my position to favor my friends and relatives. Appointing Abigail would give my enemies a pretext for more lies against me. Your Majesty is too just not to understand that.

QUEEN: *(Embarrassed and half-convinced.)* Yes...I certainly understand. But I would still like to help poor Abigail...

DUCHESS: Ah, don't worry about her. I'll find her some good position far from London. After all, she's my cousin.

QUEEN: Very well then.

DUCHESS: I am always happy when I can divine Your Majesty's intentions…as with that young ensign in the Guards whom Your Majesty commended to me the other day.

QUEEN: I did? Who was that?

DUCHESS: Young Masham, whose praises Your Majesty was singing.

QUEEN: *(Flustered.)* Oh yes, the young officer who reads me the *Gazette.*

DUCHESS: I managed to have him promoted. Nobody suspected a thing, not even my husband the marshal, who signed the promotion. This morning the new captain will come to thank Your Majesty.

QUEEN: *(Delighted.)* Ah! Masham is coming?

DUCHESS: I put him on the audience list.

QUEEN: Good! But if the newspapers are complaining about favors…

DUCHESS: It was the marshal who signed. It's a military promotion.

QUEEN: *(Sitting at the desk left.)* That's true.

DUCHESS: You see I am the first to consider your wishes.

QUEEN: *(Turning to her.)* You are so good!

DUCHESS: *(Standing by the armchair.)* No, I am simply devoted to Your Majesty. Kings have so few real friends.

QUEEN: You're right, duchess. Friendship is very precious.

(The Queen extends her hand and the Duchess kisses it.)

DUCHESS: Your Majesty promises me this ends the whole affair? It has made me so unhappy. Let it be buried and forgotten.

QUEEN: I give you my word.

DUCHESS: So it's agreed—you'll not see little Abigail again?

QUEEN: Agreed.

(Thompson comes in to announce:)

THOMPSON: Miss Abigail Churchill.

(He goes out after Abigail enters.)

DUCHESS: *(As she moves away.)* Oh hell!

QUEEN: *(Embarrassed.)* We were just speaking of you. Such a coincidence!

ABIGAIL: Your Majesty ordered me to come.

QUEEN: Well, I hardly ordered…! I said, "See if that young person…"

DUCHESS: That's right. Your Majesty is obliged to see her in order to announce that her demand cannot be granted.

ABIGAIL: My demand! I would never have dared demand! It's Her Majesty herself who, in her goodness, proposed that…

QUEEN: True enough…but political considerations…

ABIGAIL: *(Smiling.)* Political? Me?

QUEEN: …oblige me regretfully… The duchess your cousin has promised to obtain an honorable position for you…away from

London. *(With dignity she passes close by the Duchess to center stage.)* And I count on her promise.

ABIGAIL: Oh heavens!

DUCHESS: I shall see to it…at once. *(To Abigail.)* Wait for me. I'll speak to you after I see the queen to her chamber.

QUEEN: *(Softly to Abigail.)* Thank her.

(Abigail stands unmoving; but as the Duchess turns away to the door, Abigail quickly kisses the Queen's hand.)

ABIGAIL: Poor queen.

(The queen leaves with the duchess by the door right. Abigail watches them go and then sinks to her knees.)

Dear Lord, I ask nothing for myself…but let Arthur reach the continent safely. Let him live…and I'll renounce happiness.

(Bolingbroke has entered before her prayer ends.)

BOLINGBROKE: I renounce nothing. Why should you?

ABIGAIL: Oh, Lord Henry, I'm so miserable.

BOLINGBROKE: *(Cheerily.)* It's in moments like these that I arrive. Now, what's the matter?

ABIGAIL: Our luck has run out. Everything is against us.

BOLINGBROKE: On the contrary, Fortune is true to her word, prompt and punctual.

ABIGAIL: *(Puzzled.)* What do you mean?

BOLINGBROKE: Did I ever mention my cousin, Viscount Richard Bolingbroke?

ABIGAIL: I don't remember.

BOLINGBROKE: Cousin Richard was my most ruthless creditor. He sold my debts to the Duchess of Marlborough.

ABIGAIL: Another unhelpful relative!

BOLINGBROKE: And a rich one. *(Laughing.)* Look me over. Do I strike you as the heir to a fortune?

ABIGAIL: You, Lord St. John?

BOLINGBROKE: Myself in person…now Viscount Bolingbroke, the last of that illustrious family and possessor of a vast inheritance! I am here to petition for justice from the queen. *(Pointing to the door which is opening.)* Together with my honorable colleagues here, the chief members of the opposition.

ABIGAIL: Justice? For what?

BOLINGBROKE: *(Softly.)* In addition to the legacy for me, my late cousin leaves a nasty mess for the Whigs. Sh! Here's the queen.

(Abigail is at right. Several Lords and Ladies of the court take their places beside her. Members of the opposition group themselves around Bolingbroke, left. The Queen, the Duchess, and several Ladies-in-Waiting come in and gather center. Bolingbroke tries to read their expressions as he presents his case, forcing an indignation he does not feel.)

Your Majesty, as your devoted subject and as a bereaved relative, I come to ask for justice and retribution. Richard, Viscount Bolingbroke, my noble cousin, yesterday in your palace gardens…

ABIGAIL: Oh my God…

BOLINGBROKE: …was struck down in a duel—if one can call a duel a fight without witnesses from which his assailant fled.

DUCHESS: If my lord will permit…

BOLINGBROKE: How can we help but believe that those who aided his escape are those who put the sword in his hand? How can we help but believe it was the Whig ministry? *(To the Duchess and several Lords who try to speak.)* Yes, Your Majesty, I accuse—and the cries of the people are louder than mine—I accuse the Whig ministers; I accuse their partisans and their friends of treachery. If serious troubles break out in Her Majesty's capital, it is not to us, her faithful servants, she must look…but to those around her.

DUCHESS: *(Coldly.)* Have you finished?

BOLINGBROKE: I have, Your Grace.

DUCHESS: Now here is the truth about this incident, from authoritative reports I received this morning. It is unfortunately only too true that yesterday in St. James Park, Lord Richard was killed in a duel.

BOLINGBROKE: With whom?

DUCHESS: Someone whose name he did not even know.

BOLINGBROKE: I ask Your Majesty if that is very likely.

DUCHESS: That is what Lord Richard said. They were his last words, to the courtiers who found him—and who can be seen and questioned.

BOLINGBROKE: No doubt. And what kind of story these courtiers will tell we can surmise from the enviable places they occupy in the palace. But if, as Her Grace the duchess contends, the real culprit has escaped without being seen—which would presuppose an intimate knowledge of the rooms and passages of the palace— why have no measures been taken to discover him?

DUCHESS: They have.

ABIGAIL: Oh God...

DUCHESS: Her Majesty prescribes the most rigorous measures in this edict...

QUEEN: ...the execution of which we entrust to Her Grace the duchess *(Handing Bolingbroke the paper.)* and to you, Lord St. John—I should say Lord Bolingbroke—on whom your new title and the bonds of blood impose the duty of pursuing and punishing the culprit.

DUCHESS: I trust we'll hear no more about treachery.

QUEEN: My lord—and gentlemen—are you satisfied?

BOLINGBROKE: One is always satisfied when one has seen Her Majesty and heard her speak.

(With a wave of her hand the Queen salutes Bolingbroke and his colleagues, who bow low. The Queen returns with the Duchess and her Ladies to the apartments at right. The rest file out at the rear. Abigail starts to follow them; then she comes down left.)

Thanks to this edict, I can arrest all England if I choose! *(He turns to Abigail, who leans almost fainting on the back of the chair.)* My God! What's wrong?

ABIGAIL: You have ruined us.

Act II

BOLINGBROKE: How do you mean?

ABIGAIL: This culprit you swore to arrest and punish…

BOLINGBROKE: Well?

ABIGAIL: …it's Arthur!

BOLINGBROKE: What?! The duel? The fight…?

ABIGAIL: …was with your cousin, the stranger who slapped him…

BOLINGBROKE: *(With a cry.)* I see! That slap was the cause of it all—the duel, today's riots, the magnificent speech I just made…and a royal edict…

ABIGAIL: …which orders you to arrest him.

BOLINGBROKE: *(Briskly.)* Arrest him? Not likely! A man I owe so much?—a title and millions of pounds? No, no, I have not outgrown my breeches to that extent. *(Starting to tear up the edict, then stopping.)* But I have mobilized the entire opposition behind this manhunt. Richard was my relative, after all; he was my cousin.

ABIGAIL: What are you going to do?

BOLINGBROKE: *(Brightly.)* Why…nothing! A few articles in the newspaper, a few speeches…until we're sure Masham is out of England. Then I pursue him up and down the kingdom with a zeal that will do a cousin proud.

ABIGAIL: How good you are! How kind! That's wonderful! He left yesterday, so he should be far away by now… Aaaa!

(She cries out as Masham enters.)

BOLINGBROKE: *(Seeing him.)* You wretch! What brings you back to London?

MASHAM: *(Calmly.)* I never left.

ABIGAIL: But…you bade me farewell yesterday!

MASHAM: I wasn't out of the city before I heard someone galloping after me. It was a fellow officer, who soon overtook me. I thought for an instant of fighting him…but I didn't want to kill another man, one who had done me no harm… So I said, "Lieutenant, I am at your orders." "My orders are these," he said and gave me a packet of papers.

ABIGAIL: Well?

MASHAM: Can you believe it! It was my promotion to Captain of the Guards!

BOLINGBROKE: Virtue rewarded.

MASHAM: The lieutenant explained they were having a company dinner in my honor, all my comrades in the regiment. What could I do?

ABIGAIL: *(Aghast.)* You came back with him?

MASHAM: Yes. Dinner lasted half the night.

ABIGAIL: Oh, Arthur! Poor Arthur…

MASHAM: Why "poor Arthur"?

BOLINGBROKE: No time to explain. The man you fought was a cousin of mine.

Act II

MASHAM: Oh, I'm sorry.

BOLINGBROKE: Don't be. His death brought me in a lot of money. Unfortunately I've been ordered to arrest you.

MASHAM: *(Presenting his sword.)* I am at your orders.

BOLINGBROKE: Ah...no. I have no promotion to offer you...and no regimental dinner.

ABIGAIL: A good thing too, or Arthur would go right along. Thank heaven they have no suspicion it was you, Arthur.

BOLINGBROKE: Lie low; I won't look for you very hard.

MASHAM: But this morning I have to see the queen.

BOLINGBROKE: Oh damn!

MASHAM: And here's a letter ordering me to be in the palace every day.

ABIGAIL: A letter from whom?

MASHAM: My unknown protector. It came with this box...

(Thompson appears at the queen's door.)

THOMPSON: Captain Masham!

MASHAM: The queen is expecting me. *(Giving Abigail the letter and Bolingbroke the box.)* Here. Hold these.

(He and Thompson disappear into the queen's apartment.)

ABIGAIL: What's all this about?

BOLINGBROKE: Read it.

ABIGAIL: *(Reading the letter.)* "Now you are a captain! I have kept my word; keep yours and continue to obey me. Soon I shall make myself known to you. Until then, silence and obedience to my orders." What orders?—I ask you!

BOLINGBROKE: Not to marry.

ABIGAIL: Not to marry! Why?

BOLINGBROKE: *(Smiling.)* Well, this mysterious protector…

ABIGAIL: A friend of his father's! Some lord!

BOLINGBROKE: I'll wager it's a lady.

ABIGAIL: Not Arthur! He's so young! So staunch and firm and up-standing!

BOLINGBROKE: Yes… That may be the problem.

ABIGAIL: I don't understand. Perhaps this postscript will give us a clue.

BOLINGBROKE: Ah! There's a postscript?

ABIGAIL: *(Reading with rising emotion.)* "I send Captain Masham the insignia of his rank."

BOLINGBROKE: *(Opening the box.)* Diamond clips. Very tasteful. Very handsome.

ABIGAIL: *(Examining them.)* Heavens! I recognize these. They come from Mister Tomwood's. I sold them myself, last week.

BOLINGBROKE: Who bought them? Tell me!

ABIGAIL: Oh, I dare not. It was a very great lady, and I am lost if she is in love with Arthur.

BOLINGBROKE: What do you care—if he's not in love with her! He doesn't even suspect…!

ABIGAIL: He'll know soon enough. I'm going to tell him.

BOLINGBROKE: *(Taking her hand.)* No…if you follow my advice…he'll never find out.

ABIGAIL: Why not?

BOLINGBROKE: My poor child! You don't know men. The most modest of them are so vain! It's flattering, you know, to be loved by a great lady. And if it's true that this one is so powerful…

ABIGAIL: More than I can tell you.

BOLINGBROKE: Who is she?

(The Duchess is entering from the gallery right.)

ABIGAIL: Here she is…

(Bolingbroke takes the letter from Abigail.)

BOLINGBROKE: *(Brightening.)* The duchess? *(Urging Abigail to go.)* Leave us, leave us.

ABIGAIL: She told me to wait.

BOLINGBROKE: *(Taking her toward the door left.)* Well, she'll find me instead. Fortune owes me this one.

(The Duchess is looking thoughtful. Bolingbroke approaches and bows respectfully.)

DUCHESS: Oh, it's you, my lord. I was expecting that young woman.

BOLINGBROKE: Dare I ask for a moment of your time?

DUCHESS: Do you have some clue to the culprit?

BOLINGBROKE: None as yet. Do you, Your Grace?

DUCHESS: Nothing at all.

BOLINGBROKE: Then we're even.

DUCHESS: Well, what do you want?

BOLINGBROKE: First, to pay off my debts. I'll remit a million to your banker to repay the hundred thousand or so you considered them worth.

DUCHESS: My lord…

BOLINGBROKE: Oh, that was a lot! I wouldn't have paid that much. You'll make several hundred percent profit—not a bad bit of business.

DUCHESS: It is for you.

BOLINGBROKE: Oh no, Your Grace. It taught me something very valuable—that a statesman needs discipline. Discipline leads to wealth, and wealth leads to power. With money, one does not have to sell out…and often one can buy up others. That lesson was worth a million.

DUCHESS: I understand. Now that you need not fear debtors' prison, you intend all-out war on me.

BOLINGBROKE: On the contrary, I come to propose peace.

DUCHESS: Peace between you and me? That would be difficult.

BOLINGBROKE: Well, a truce. A truce for twenty-four hours.

DUCHESS: Why? You've forced me to acknowledge Abigail as a relative of mine and put the girl in a royal residence—thirty leagues from here.

BOLINGBROKE: That's very generous, but I doubt that she'll accept.

DUCHESS: Why not?

BOLINGBROKE: She wants to stay in London.

DUCHESS: *(Ironically.)* Because of you perhaps?

BOLINGBROKE: *(Fatuously.)* Possibly.

DUCHESS: *(Smiling.)* Really now, my lord, are you in love with that little thing? At your age?

BOLINGBROKE: Supposing I were?

DUCHESS: I'd be delighted. A statesman in love is lost! He's vulnerable.

BOLINGBROKE: I don't see that. I know very able politicians who balance affairs of the heart with affairs of State. Among others I know a great lady—you know her too—who is so charmed by the youth and innocence of a gentleman from the provinces that she takes pleasure in being his invisible protector, and without ever revealing her identity, has taken charge of his advancement. *(At an involuntary movement from the Duchess.)* Interesting, isn't it, Your Grace? Recently through her husband, who is a famous marshal, she has had her protégé made Captain of the Guards; and this very morning she cunningly informed him of his new rank by sending him his insignia—done in diamonds that are quite magnificent, they say.

DUCHESS: *(Uncomfortably.)* That hardly seems likely. And how can you be sure?

BOLINGBROKE: Here they are! Also the letter that accompanied them. *(Quietly.)* You understand this is only between the two of us, because this secret could ruin the great lady. Promotions like this young man's are subject to approval by the Commons, including the opposition. You may say that the great lady might survive the frightful publicity…but she has a husband—this marshal I mentioned—with a terrible temper. He hates scandal.

DUCHESS: *(Angry.)* My lord!

BOLINGBROKE: *(A change in tone.)* Your Grace, let's talk business. You understand I cannot hold these proofs forever. I must return them.

DUCHESS: Ah, if that's true…

BOLINGBROKE: Between you and me—no promises, only actions! Tomorrow Abigail will be appointed to the queen's household, here, in London…and all this will be returned to you.

DUCHESS: Now.

BOLINGBROKE: No—only when Abigail enters upon her duties. And it will depend on you whether that is tomorrow…or this evening.

DUCHESS: You doubt my word?

BOLINGBROKE: Shouldn't I?

DUCHESS: You really hate me, don't you?

BOLINGBROKE: *(Gallantly.)* No! I find you charming! And if instead of being opponents fate had joined us, we might have ruled the world!

DUCHESS: You think so? How did you discover all this?

BOLINGBROKE: I'm a journalist. I can't tell you that without compromising a source.

DUCHESS: You're rich now and you bribed one of my people—let's say William, my private secretary.

BOLINGBROKE: *(Smiling.)* That's possible.

DUCHESS: The only one on my staff I trusted!

BOLINGBROKE: Then, that's the end of William.

DUCHESS: The end of them all!

BOLINGBROKE: This evening—the appointment of Abigail…

DUCHESS: This evening—that letter!

BOLINGBROKE: I pledge truce for today, frank and open.

DUCHESS: So be it! *(She extends her hand and Bolingbroke raises it to his lips.)* And tomorrow—war! *(She leaves at the right and Bolingbroke at the left.)*

END OF ACT TWO

ACT III

Scene: The same. Afternoon two days later.

At Rise: Abigail, holding a book, and the Queen her tapestry needle-work enter from the door right. The Queen sits near the table right, and Abigail stands by her chair.

ABIGAIL: I cannot get over my good fortune. Me, Abigail, permitted to attend Your Majesty!

QUEEN: It wasn't easy to achieve, but I always prevail. I may seem to yield, and sometimes I do; but at the first opportunity I show my true character—as I did two days ago!

ABIGAIL: You must have spoken to the duchess like a…like a queen!

QUEEN: *(Naively.)* No, I didn't say a word. But she could tell I was not pleased…and she came to me, so embarrassed, to confess that my will was too strong for her. Just to punish her, I hesitated for an instant…and then I told her decisively I wanted you here!

ABIGAIL: You're so good to me. Would Your Majesty like me to read?

(The Queen indicates she is ready to listen. Abigail finds a tabouret, places it near the Queen, and opens the book.)

"History of Parliament."

(The Queen, with a gesture of boredom, places a hand over the open book.)

QUEEN: I needed someone like you, Abigail. With you I can think out loud. I'm not queen any longer. I'm not…bored.

ABIGAIL: Queens can be bored?

Act III

(The Queen takes the book from Abigail and tosses it on the table.)

QUEEN: Bored to death! Especially in England... Busy all day with dull papers...and people who are so sure of themselves. With them I listen...with you I chat. You are such a...happy person!

ABIGAIL: Not always. Sometimes I feel quite sad.

QUEEN: Ah! there is a kind of sadness I don't mind...like yesterday, for instance, when we were talking about my brother. They have exiled poor Jamie and I may never see him again...except by an act of Parliament I may never get. Me! The queen!

ABIGAIL: That's terrible.

QUEEN: Yes, isn't it? And while I was talking I saw tears in your eyes and I knew I had a friend.

ABIGAIL: They are right to call you Good Queen Anne.

QUEEN: Yes, I am good and people take advantage of it. They all want something.

ABIGAIL: Well, give others the honors and share your troubles with me.

(The Queen rises and tosses her needlework on the table.)

QUEEN: Troubles are my entire life. We Stuarts are all exiles...poor Jamie in France and I on this throne.

ABIGAIL: You are young...and free, as you said. Why remain alone?

QUEEN: Give myself to a husband chosen by Parliament? No, no, I prefer solitude to slavery.

ABIGAIL: A queen cannot choose for herself...whom to love?

QUEEN: No, indeed.

ABIGAIL: Not even in dreams?

QUEEN: *(Smiling.)* Parliament forbids it. But there is a dream I have though no one will ever know it.

ABIGAIL: Why not? You can whisper the name of your hero and I will never tell.

QUEEN: *(Smiling.)* I'm not telling either.

ABIGAIL: It's some handsome lord, I'm sure.

QUEEN: Perhaps! All I know is that for three months I've scarcely said a word to him…and he has never said a word to me!

ABIGAIL: Why ever not?

QUEEN: It's very simple: I'm the queen…

ABIGAIL: But when we're alone you can talk about your hero…with no fear of Parliament.

QUEEN: Yes! Oh, that's what I like about you, Abigail—you are not always talking about affairs of State. You never do.

ABIGAIL: Oh! Heavens!

QUEEN: What's the matter?

ABIGAIL: That's exactly what I must talk to you about! I was forgetting something Lord Bolingbroke confided to me and Captain Masham.

QUEEN: *(With some emotion.)* Masham?

Act III

ABIGAIL: The officer on duty today. You see, ma'am, Bolingbroke once met in France a worthy gentleman who was of great service to him, and he wanted to help this friend by getting him...

QUEEN: A position? A title?

ABIGAIL: No, an audience with Your Majesty...or at least an invitation to this evening's soirée.

QUEEN: The duchess is in charge of invitations. I'll give her his name. *(Sitting at the desk.)* Who is he?

ABIGAIL: The Marquis de Torcy.

QUEEN: *(Quickly.)* Hush!

ABIGAIL: Why? What's the matter?

QUEEN: The *marquis* is a nobleman I esteem, but he is an envoy of Louis XIV, and if the duchess knew that you have spoken up for him...

ABIGAIL: Well?

QUEEN: Well! It would bring on all kinds of lectures! And if I *saw* the *marquis*...

ABIGAIL: But Lord Bolingbroke says you must see him! And you are the queen... You'd like to see him, wouldn't you?

QUEEN: *(Uncomfortably.)* Certainly I'd...like to...

ABIGAIL: Then you agree?

QUEEN: It's just that... Quiet!

(The Duchess enters at the rear.)

DUCHESS: Here are the dispatches from the marshal. In spite of... *(She stops on seeing Abigail.)*

QUEEN: Well? Go on.

DUCHESS: I'll wait until the young lady has gone.

ABIGAIL: Does Your Majesty command me to leave?

QUEEN: *(Embarrassed.)* No... I have some instructions for you... *(With affected severity.)* Meanwhile take a book. *(Graciously.)* Well, duchess?

DUCHESS: *(In ill humor.)* In spite of Bolingbroke's speech, Parliament will approve subsidies for the army on condition that we renounce all negotiations with Louis XIV.

QUEEN: Yes, of course.

DUCHESS: The French ambassador's presence in London is intolerable. I promised in your name that you would not see the Marquis de Torcy and this very day he would be given his passports.

ABIGAIL: *(Dropping her book.)* Oh heavens!

DUCHESS: What's the matter with you?

ABIGAIL: *(With an imploring look at the queen.)* This book...it fell.

QUEEN: It seems to me we might hear what the *marquis* has to say...

DUCHESS: Parliament would turn against us. Bolingbroke will see to that. Of course, if Your Majesty wants to risk the ugly riots that will follow...

Act III

QUEEN: *(Frightened and vexed.)* Oh heavens, no! We have had more than enough riots already. *(She goes to sit at the table left.)*

DUCHESS: Good... I'll write a letter of dismissal to the *marquis* and bring it to Your Majesty for your signature.

QUEEN: Very well.

DUCHESS: Here...at three o'clock, when I come to take you to the chapel.

QUEEN: Wonderful. I thank you.

(The Duchess leaves. Abigail is still sitting with her book at the table.)

ABIGAIL: Poor Marquis de Torcy! No peace treaty now.

(She replaces the tabouret near the rear door. The Queen is at left going over the dispatches.)

QUEEN: Ah! What a bore...these dispatches from the marshal...as if I understood military terms!

(She peruses the report. Masham appears at the rear, near Abigail.)

ABIGAIL: Oh my God! What is it?

MASHAM: *(In a low voice.)* A note from our friend and ally.

ABIGAIL: *(Taking it.)* From Lord Henry?

MASHAM: He's downstairs waiting for you.

ABIGAIL: *(Reading.)* "Tell the queen about your marriage plans." *(To Masham.)* You tell her. I'll go to him.

(She runs out at rear. Masham starts to follow. The Queen turns at the sound of his footsteps.)

QUEEN: What is it? Oh, it's you, Captain Masham!

MASHAM: Yes, ma'am.

QUEEN: Is there something you wanted?

MASHAM: A…a word with Your Majesty.

QUEEN: Good! You never ask for anything. You never even speak!

MASHAM: That's true, ma'am, but today…

QUEEN: What emboldens you now?

MASHAM: Some difficulties I'm in. If Your Majesty could spare me a few minutes…

QUEEN: I have dispatches to read…

MASHAM: *(Respectfully.)* I'll go then.

QUEEN: No! Don't do that! I…I must be fair to my subjects. I must hear their appeals. Yours no doubt is about your rank?

MASHAM: No, ma'am.

QUEEN: A title? Another promotion?

MASHAM: Oh no, ma'am. I'm not here about that.

QUEEN: *(Smiling.)* Then why are you here?

Act III

MASHAM: Ma'am, I fear it might be lacking in respect to burden Your Majesty with my personal affairs...

QUEEN: *(Lightly.)* Why? I love secrets. Tell me, I beg of you. *(Extending her hand to him.)* You may count in advance on our royal protection.

MASHAM: *(Her hand to his lips.)* Oh, ma'am...!

QUEEN: *(Moved, drawing back her hand.)* Well?

MASHAM: Well, ma'am, I already have a powerful protector...

QUEEN: *(With a gesture of surprise.)* Oh, really...!

MASHAM: That surprises you?

QUEEN: No... It doesn't surprise me.

MASHAM: This mysterious protector absolutely forbids me...

QUEEN: Forbids you what?

MASHAM: To marry.

QUEEN: *(Laughing.)* Forbids you to marry! You of all people! That is strange! *(Curiously.)* Go on, go on...

(Abigail enters and the Queen turns on her in indignation.)

Now what is it? Who intrudes like this? Oh, it's you, Abigail. I'll speak to you later.

ABIGAIL: Oh, ma'am—at once, if you please! A friend, a devoted friend must see Your Majesty without delay.

QUEEN: *(Irritated.)* Always interrupted…never an instant for important matters! What do they want of me? What sort of person is this?

ABIGAIL: Lord Bolingbroke.

QUEEN: *(Rising in alarm.)* Lord Henry?

ABIGAIL: It's a matter of the gravest importance, he says.

QUEEN: He can't come in here! The duchess will *see* him!

ABIGAIL: Then quickly, before she returns!

QUEEN: An interview with Lord Henry would do no good now.

ABIGAIL: Then see him and tell him so…because I instructed them to send him up.

QUEEN: With the duchess here at any minute? And bound to run into him? What have you done?

ABIGAIL: Punish me, ma'am. Here he is!

QUEEN: *(Crossing away in anger.)* Leave us.

(Bolingbroke has entered at the rear.)

ABIGAIL: *(To him.)* She's furious.

MASHAM: *(Adding.)* And you'll waste your breath.

BOLINGBROKE: We'll see. Who knows…with a little luck…

(Abigail and Masham leave. The Queen is sitting near the table right. Bolingbroke approaches her and bows low.)

Act III

QUEEN: Lord Henry, at any other time I'd be delighted to see you...

BOLINGBROKE: I come to plead for England...and the Marquis de Torcy.

QUEEN: It's useless; the *marquis'* passports are being prepared this very moment.

BOLINGBROKE: But they aren't signed yet! If he leaves, the war will only intensify. There'll be no end in sight. Hear me out...

QUEEN: It's all decided. I'm expecting the duchess with the papers at three o'clock. If she finds you here...

BOLINGBROKE: Ma'am, it's not yet three. Will you at least give me the few minutes that remain?

(As the queen drops into her armchair.)

A quarter of an hour, ma'am—that's all the time left for me to show you the misery of this country—her trade destroyed, her debts mounting by the hour...because of a war that's ruining us. Ma'am, do you know that the capture of Bouchain cost England seven million pounds sterling?

QUEEN: Permit me, my lord!

BOLINGBROKE: *(Continuing.)* Do you know that at Malplaquet we lost thirty thousand soldiers and the French only eight thousand?

QUEEN: Lord Henry, you want peace; I know that. And you may be right. But I am only a woman, and I must choose between you and others who are also devoted to me.

BOLINGBROKE: *(Bristling.)* They are deceiving you! I'll prove it.

QUEEN: I'd rather not know. I'd have to be angry, and I haven't the strength.

BOLINGBROKE: Ma'am, if it were proved to you beyond any doubt that a good part of our subsidies goes straight into the pocket of the Duke of Marlborough—which is his motive for continuing the war...

QUEEN: *(Listening.)* Sh! I thought I heard... Go now, Lord Henry. They're coming.

BOLINGBROKE: No, ma'am. If I added that the duchess dreads an end to the war too, because it would bring her husband back to London...

QUEEN: I'll never believe that.

BOLINGBROKE: It's the truth! The young captain who was just here, Arthur Masham, could give you more exact details.

QUEEN: Masham? What do you mean?

BOLINGBROKE: The duchess is in love with him.

QUEEN: *(Trembling.)* With Masham?

BOLINGBROKE: *(About to leave.)* With him...among others. But that doesn't matter.

QUEEN: Doesn't matter! *(Rising.)* If I am being deceived...! If I am being betrayed...! No, no! This must be explained. Stay here, my lord, stay right here. I am the queen and I intend to know everything. *(She goes to look off into the gallery right.)*

BOLINGBROKE: *(To himself.)* Is Masham by any chance...? Does the destiny of England lie in that youngster's lap?

QUEEN: *(Returning.)* You were saying that the duchess...

BOLINGBROKE: *(Looking intently into her face.)* ...wants the war to go on...

QUEEN: ...to keep her husband away from London.

BOLINGBROKE: Yes, ma'am.

QUEEN: Out of love for Masham.

BOLINGBROKE: I have reasons to believe so.

QUEEN: What reasons?

BOLINGBROKE: First, it was the duchess who got him a position in Your Majesty's household.

QUEEN: That's true!

BOLINGBROKE: She had him breveted as ensign.

QUEEN: That's true!

BOLINGBROKE: Through her a few days later he was commissioned Captain of the Guards.

QUEEN: Yes, under the pretext that I wanted him myself—desired...it...myself. And that mysterious protector Masham told me about...

BOLINGBROKE: Or protectress.

QUEEN: ...who forbade him to marry...

BOLINGBROKE: *(In her ear.)* It was the duchess. To be free for such romantic escapades, the noble duchess keeps her husband in the field and has Parliament vote subsidies to carry on the war! *(With emphasis.)* A war which brings the Marlboroughs glory and money and pleasure—pleasure all the greater because it is secret and allows her to laugh up her sleeve at the royal personages who serve her ambitions...and her amours!

(At an angry gesture from the queen.)

Yes, ma'am.

QUEEN: Silence. Here she is.

(The Duchess sails in at the door right. She sees Bolingbroke with the Queen and is thunderstruck.)

DUCHESS: Bolingbroke!

(He bows. The Queen, who tries to conceal her anger throughout the scene, speaks coldly:)

QUEEN: What is it, Your Grace? What do you want?

DUCHESS: *(Presenting papers.)* Passports and letter of dismissal for the Marquis de Torcy.

QUEEN: *(Drily.)* Very well. *(She tosses the papers on the desk.)*

DUCHESS: I brought them for Your Majesty to sign.

(The Queen goes to the desk left and sits.)

QUEEN: Very well! I'll read them. I'll examine them.

DUCHESS: But Your Majesty—Your Majesty had already decided he must go this very day.

QUEEN: Yes…I had. But new developments oblige me to reconsider.

DUCHESS: *(Looking angrily at Bolingbroke.)* I can easily guess why Your Majesty is now yielding…

QUEEN: *(Struggling to contain herself.)* What do you mean? I yield only to reason and justice.

BOLINGBROKE: *(Standing at the queen's right.)* We know everything.

QUEEN: The truth may be kept from me…but once I know it…I no longer hesitate.

BOLINGBROKE: Spoken like a queen.

QUEEN: The capture of Bouchain cost England seven million pounds sterling!

DUCHESS: Ma'am?

QUEEN: *(More and more animated.)* All told, at Malplaquet we lost thirty thousand fighting men!

DUCHESS: But…permit me…

QUEEN: *(Rising.)* And you want me to sign that…without knowing exactly for myself? No, duchess, I refuse to sacrifice the interests of the State to the ambitions of others.

DUCHESS: Allow me one word…

QUEEN: I cannot. It's time to go to chapel.

(Abigail has entered right. To her:)

Come, let's go.

ABIGAIL: Your Majesty is upset.

QUEEN: *(With quiet urgency.)* That person we talked about…? I must see him.

ABIGAIL: *(Lightly.)* Who? The dream hero?

QUEEN: Yes. Bring him to me.

ABIGAIL: For that, I'd have to know who he is!

(The Queen turns and sees Masham, who has just entered rear and now offers the Queen her gloves and Bible.)

QUEEN: *(Softly to Abigail.)* Here he is now.

ABIGAIL: *(Immobile with surprise.)* Oh my God!

BOLINGBROKE: *(In passing.)* It's going superbly.

ABIGAIL: We're lost.

BOLINGBROKE: We've won!

(The Queen has taken the gloves and the Bible from Masham. She signals Abigail to follow her. Both move off. The Duchess angrily snatches the papers from the desk and leaves. Bolingbroke watches her in triumph.)

END OF ACT THREE

ACT IV

Scene: The same.

At Rise: The Duchess alone, muttering to herself. Now and then a salient phrase becomes clear.

DUCHESS: I refuse, she says! *(Laughing.)* Unheard of!

(Masham enters warily and bows respectfully.)

Well, we'll see! *(She becomes aware of Masham's presence.)* Ah, Masham. You were recently promoted to Captain of the Guards.

MASHAM: Yes, Your Grace.

DUCHESS: By the Duke of Marlborough. What entitles you to such a promotion?

MASHAM: Not my merit, certainly. Perhaps my ardor and devotion.

DUCHESS: "Ardor and devotion." I like that answer. I see why you were promoted.

MASHAM: I only wish the duke would grant me another favor.

DUCHESS: He will, I'm sure. Name it.

MASHAM: He will? Truly?

DUCHESS: What is it you would like?

MASHAM: I am a soldier. I want to see action!

DUCHESS: You'd like a tussle would you? Some rough-and-tumble? I'll see you get it, take my word.

MASHAM: Your Grace is so good! They told me you were my enemy!

DUCHESS: Who did?

MASHAM: Those who don't know you yet. Now they will share my devotion to you.

DUCHESS: This devotion…can I count on it?

MASHAM: Just tell me what you desire!

DUCHESS: Well…I like you, Captain. Come closer.

MASHAM: Your Grace?

DUCHESS: You hear what I say?

MASHAM: Yes, Your Grace.

DUCHESS: I have something in mind…and I think you are just the man for the job. You will report to me every day…what's up… and we'll discuss ways to uncover the culprit.

MASHAM: Uncover the culprit?

DUCHESS: Yes. I'm itching to get my hands on the rascal.

MASHAM: I don't understand.

DUCHESS: *(Losing patience.)* A crime has been committed here in the palace! Richard Bolingbroke has been assassinated!

MASHAM: *(Indignantly.)* Not assassinated, Your Grace. The pig died sword in hand fighting a gentleman he had insulted.

DUCHESS: You know his assailant? Tell me. I have sworn to pursue him.

Act IV

MASHAM: Look no further, Your Grace. I am the man.

DUCHESS: You, Masham!

MASHAM: Yes, Your Grace. I did it. And I'm glad.

DUCHESS: *(Putting her hand over his mouth.)* Hush! Hush! Nobody must know! I find no fault in you…personally…whatever comes up…when I get my hands on…the culprit… But enemies might say your promotion was a reward…for…

MASHAM: Sticking this pig? That's true.

DUCHESS: There's one way to save you. You leave for the battlefield tomorrow.

MASHAM: Action at last! Ah, how can I ever thank you! Just tell me!

DUCHESS: *(Warmly.)* I know a way. I have some dispatches for the duke. You must come to my rooms and get them.

MASHAM: When?

DUCHESS: Tonight, after the queen's soirée. And so no one will suspect, take care not to be seen.

MASHAM: I will. But I still can't get over it. You—I was so afraid of! Now I feel…I feel I must reveal everything to you!

DUCHESS: *(Tenderly.)* You do that tonight. Now hush! Someone's coming.

(Abigail, much upset, enters right.)

That Abigail is everywhere! What do you want?

ABIGAIL: *(Troubled, looking at the two of them.)* Nothing. I was afraid… *(Recovering.)* Oh yes, I remember. The queen wishes to speak to Your Grace.

DUCHESS: Very well. I'll go to her later.

ABIGAIL: This minute, Your Grace. The queen is waiting.

DUCHESS: You can say to your mistress…

ABIGAIL: *(With dignity.)* I have nothing to say to anyone…except to Your Grace, to whom I have delivered the orders of my mistress—and yours.

(The Duchess looks angry enough to burst but contains her choler and goes out.)

MASHAM: What are you thinking of, Abigail! Speaking to her like that!

ABIGAIL: Why do you defend her?

MASHAM: Because of all she's done for us! You told me she was imperious…

ABIGAIL: …and wicked! I said it and I say it again!

MASHAM: You're wrong. You don't know how much I owe her.

ABIGAIL: What!?

MASHAM: I told her about my duel with Richard Bolingbroke and she generously promised to protect me.

ABIGAIL: How much protection do you need?

Act IV

MASHAM: *(Astonished.)* Abigail! I don't recognize you! What's all this… emotion?

ABIGAIL: It's the damned duchess! What did she say to you?

MASHAM: She wants to keep me out of danger…

ABIGAIL: Keep you out of danger. I see.

MASHAM: …so she's sending me to the battlefield.

(Abigail screams.)

ABIGAIL: She wants to kill you! And you think that woman loves you? I mean…wants to…to protect you?

MASHAM: She does! Tonight she's giving me dispatches in her room.

ABIGAIL: Giving you what?

MASHAM: Dispatches. In her room.

ABIGAIL: And you're going?

MASHAM: Of course I'm going. She was so friendly! When you came in I was about to tell her of our plans to marry.

ABIGAIL: *(Melting.)* Arthur! That's very sweet!

MASHAM: And tonight in her room I'll certainly tell her.

ABIGAIL: No! No, don't go. Find an excuse.

MASHAM: She'll be offended and we'll be lost.

ABIGAIL: Never mind. It's better so.

MASHAM: Why?

ABIGAIL: Because the queen wants you at her soirée. She wishes to talk to you.

MASHAM: Oh. Then I'll go see the queen instead.

ABIGAIL: No! You won't do that either!

MASHAM: Why not?

ABIGAIL: I can't tell you. Take pity on me, Arthur! I'm in torment!

MASHAM: How do you mean?

ABIGAIL: Listen to me, Arthur. Do you love me as I love you?

MASHAM: More than my life.

ABIGAIL: That's what I wanted to hear. Now give me your word to do as I say without asking why.

MASHAM: I swear.

ABIGAIL: To begin with, never ever speak of our marriage to the duchess.

MASHAM: You're right. First I'd better tell the queen.

ABIGAIL: That's even worse!

MASHAM: But when I was with the queen this morning, she looked so interested…

ABIGAIL: I'm sure she was, but…

MASHAM: She gave me her beautiful hand to hold and I kissed it. —
What's the matter? Yours is icy.

ABIGAIL: Arthur, I'm in great favor with the queen too. But it would
have been better for both of us to remain poor and humble than
to come here to court with all its dangers and seductions.

MASHAM: *(Bristling.)* Seductions! Someone's trying to seduce you?

ABIGAIL: No…not me exactly.

(Knocking at the door left.)

Quiet, someone's knocking. It must be Lord Henry. I asked him
to come. He's the only one I can trust. Leave me alone with him.

MASHAM: Alone? Are you sure…?

ABIGAIL: Arthur. You promised to obey me.

MASHAM: Well…be careful. Remember—danger and seduction.

*(He kisses her hand and leaves at the rear. Another knocking at the
door left.)*

ABIGAIL: Oh! Lord Henry! I'm losing my mind!

(She goes to the door and admits Bolingbroke.)

BOLINGBROKE: *(Briskly.)* I hasten to pay my respects to the new
favorite. I told you so!

ABIGAIL: Yes, the queen adores me. But help me before all is lost.

BOLINGBROKE: What's the matter? Is it the Marquis de Torcy?

ABIGAIL: *(Striking her forehead.)* Oh that's right! The duchess brought his passports to the queen and she signed them. But…

BOLINGBROKE: The ambassador's being deported?

ABIGAIL: …have you heard about Arthur?

BOLINGBROKE: The *marquis* is ordered to leave London?

ABIGAIL: In twenty-four hours. Did you know Arthur is…?

BOLINGBROKE: It's all the duchess's doing.

ABIGAIL: Not just the duchess! There's something even worse!

BOLINGBROKE: Something worse for the *marquis?*

ABIGAIL: For Arthur!

BOLINGBROKE: Deliver me from people in love! I'm talking to you about war and peace and the fate for Europe!

ABIGAIL: And I'm talking about me! Europe can take care of itself!

BOLINGBROKE: Pardon, my child. Ambition is self-centered, like love. You say the queen has signed…?

ABIGAIL: *(Impatiently.)* Yes, because of some bill about her brother.

BOLINGBROKE: The queen has made peace with the duchess?

ABIGAIL: Not really. She's furious with her but she won't say why.

BOLINGBROKE: Good. An explosion just waiting for the spark. Did you remind her that if the *marquis* is leaving tomorrow, there's no risk in seeing him today? Did you tell her that?

ABIGAIL: I was thinking about something else.

BOLINGBROKE: *(Sighing.)* Very well, let's hear about something else, whatever it is.

ABIGAIL: This morning I was worried because the duchess had ideas about…protecting Arthur. Well, that was nothing! Someone else…another great lady I cannot name…

BOLINGBROKE: You poor child! How did you find out?

ABIGAIL: Don't ask me.

BOLINGBROKE: The…other great lady also loves Arthur?

ABIGAIL: *(Nodding.)* And it's not right! They have princes and dukes to choose from. All I have is Arthur. How can a poor girl keep all these great ladies off him?

BOLINGBROKE: The more the better. Two are less dangerous than one.

ABIGAIL: How can you say that?

BOLINGBROKE: When a great empire wants to conquer a tiny country, there are no obstacles. The country's done for! But let another great empire want the same country and there is a chance. The two mighty powers watch each other like cats. They counter— they neutralize each other; and the threatened country escapes… thanks to the number of its enemies. Understand?

ABIGAIL: No! Arthur's in danger! The duchess is expecting him in her rooms tonight after the queen's soirée!

BOLINGBROKE: Good! Very good!

ABIGAIL: It is not! It's very bad!

BOLINGBROKE: That's what I meant.

ABIGAIL: At the same time, the—the other person, the other great lady wants him with her, at the same hour.

BOLINGBROKE: What did I tell you? They cancel each other out. He can't go to both!

ABIGAIL: He'll go to neither—if I have my way! Luckily this other great lady won't know till the last minute if…if she will be free…for reasons I can't explain.

BOLINGBROKE: *(Straight-faced.)* I see. She's being watched.

ABIGAIL: *(Gratefully.)* Yes! And if she succeeds in removing all obstacles…

BOLINGBROKE: She'll succeed, you can be sure of that.

ABIGAIL: …then, as a signal to me and Arthur, in front of everybody she will ask casually for a glass of water.

BOLINGBROKE: Which will mean: "I'm expecting you. Come."

ABIGAIL: Exactly. I haven't told Arthur about the signal because I don't want him going anywhere!

BOLINGBROKE: How does Arthur feel about all this?

ABIGAIL: You mean—should I ruin his prospects, especially now when he might be discovered and arrested? Should I? Tell me.

BOLINGBROKE: *(Lost in thought.)* Leave it to me. The Marquis de Torcy will have an invitation tonight. He will speak with the queen.

ABIGAIL: *(Exasperated.)* The *marquis*!

BOLINGBROKE: Don't worry, Masham is safe too. I'll prevent both these rendezvous.

ABIGAIL: Ah, Lord Henry! I'll owe you my entire life! Somebody's coming. They mustn't see you. Go! Go!

BOLINGBROKE: *(Coolly.)* I've already been seen.

(The Duchess comes from the apartment at right. She bows ironically to Abigail, who returns the bow and leaves. Bolingbroke remains where he was.)

Well, the ties of blood finally prevail! You two cousins come together! It's very touching—and gives me hope for myself.

DUCHESS: Yes, you predicted you and I would end up on loving terms.

BOLINGBROKE: *(Gallantly.)* I've already begun. How about Your Grace?

DUCHESS: I've only got as far as admiration for your audacity.

BOLINGBROKE: And my dependability? I've kept all my promises.

DUCHESS: And I've kept mine! I have appointed that person to her post with the queen, where she can spy on me for you.

BOLINGBROKE: Nothing escapes you.

DUCHESS: At least I see through you. On your orders Miss Abigail tried to get the Marquis de Torcy invited to the queen's soirée.

BOLINGBROKE: My mistake. I should have gone straight to Your Grace. *(Taking a printed invitation from the desk.)* You must have an invitation here to give me for the *marquis.*

DUCHESS: *(Laughing.)* You think so?

BOLINGBROKE: In exchange for a greater favor, of course. That's the only way you and I can do business. Every advantage goes to you—seven hundred percent profit…as on my debts.

DUCHESS: What have you got—another letter? So have I—a bundle of them. Charming letters from your wife. Love letters to Lord Evandale. *(Quietly and confidentially.)* Very graphic love letters. I got them from Lord Evandale himself.

BOLINGBROKE: At discount, no doubt. Never mind, I have some helpful news for you.

DUCHESS: *(Ironically.)* Helpful? But is it pleasant?

BOLINGBROKE: I'm afraid not. That's why I give it to you. *(Quietly.)* You have a rival!

DUCHESS: *(Quickly.)* What do you mean?

BOLINGBROKE: There's a lady at court who has plans for young Masham. I have the proof. I know the time, the place, and the signal for their rendezvous.

DUCHESS: *(Trembling with rage.)* You're lying.

BOLINGBROKE: *(Coolly.)* I'm telling you true…as true as his rendezvous with you tonight after the queen's soirée.

DUCHESS: Oh hell!

BOLINGBROKE: This other rendezvous is doubtless meant to prevent yours…to snatch him from under your nose. Goodbye, Your Grace.

Act IV

(He starts out left. The Duchess follows him as far as the desk left.)

DUCHESS: The signal for this rendezvous—what is it?

(Bolingbroke presents her with the pen from the desk.)

BOLINGBROKE: First...the invitation for the Marquis de Torcy.

(The Duchess sits and writes convulsively.)

A formal invitation, according the *marquis* full honors as envoy of His Majesty King Louis XIV. Of course you are still free to continue the war against France...as you do against me.

(The invitation folded and sealed, he rings. Thompson appears and Bolingbroke gives him the invitation.)

This is to go to the Marquis de Torcy at the French Embassy across from the palace.

(Thompson bows and goes.)

The *marquis* will have it in five minutes.

DUCHESS: Well, my lord? Who is this woman?

BOLINGBROKE: She'll be here this evening, at the queen's soirée.

DUCHESS: Lady Albemarle! I'm sure of it. Or Lady Elworth...

BOLINGBROKE: I don't know her name, but we'll soon know who she is. If she can evade those around her, if she is free, if the rendezvous with Masham can take place tonight, here is the signal agreed upon...

DUCHESS: *(Impatiently.)* Well? Hurry up, for God's sake!

BOLINGBROKE: This lady will ask Masham for a glass of water.

DUCHESS: That's it? Here? Tonight?

BOLINGBROKE: Yes. You'll see for yourself.

DUCHESS: Damn them! I'll show them no mercy!

BOLINGBROKE: That's what I count on.

DUCHESS: I'll expose them before the entire court!

BOLINGBROKE: Quiet. Here are the queen and her ladies.

(The Queen, Lady Albemarle, and the Ladies-in-Waiting enter at the door right. Lords and Members of Parliament enter at the rear. The titled Ladies form a circle and sit at right. Abigail and a few Maids of Honor stand behind them. Downstage left Bolingbroke and some Members of the Opposition. At right the Duchess keeping an eye on the ladies. Behind her, Masham and some Officers.)

DUCHESS: *(To the queen as she approaches.)* I'll have the card table prepared for Your Majesty.

QUEEN: *(Looking for Masham.)* Good.

DUCHESS: The table for the queen! *(Softly to the queen.)* For the sake of form, I thought it best to invite the Marquis de Torcy.

QUEEN: *(Still looking for Masham.)* Very good.

DUCHESS: That will silence the opposition.

QUEEN: *(Spotting Masham.)* And please Abigail.

DUCHESS: Yes, indeed.

(The Duchess supervises setting up table and chairs for the card game. Meanwhile a Member of Parliament approaches the Bolingbroke group.)

MEMBER OF PARLIAMENT: Well, gentlemen, I hear negotiations for peace have been broken off.

BOLINGBROKE: Really?

MEMBER OF PARLIAMENT: The duchess is so opposed to peace that the French ambassador is not invited tonight.

BOLINGBROKE: Can you imagine?

MEMBER OF PARLIAMENT: The *marquis* must leave the country tomorrow without once seeing the queen.

THOMPSON: His Excellency the Ambassador of France, the Marquis de Torcy.

(The surprise is general. Everyone bows or curtsies to de Torcy. Bolingbroke goes to him and leads him to the queen.)

QUEEN: My lord ambassador, you are most welcome. We are very pleased to see you.

DUCHESS: *(Softly to the queen.)* For heaven's sake, not too cordial.

QUEEN: *(To Bolingbroke on her other side.)* I knew this invitation would please you. I go out of my way to do what I can.

BOLINGBROKE: *(Bowing.)* You are too good, ma'am.

DE TORCY: *(Softly to Bolingbroke.)* I just this moment received the invitation.

BOLINGBROKE: I know.

DE TORCY: Things going well?

BOLINGBROKE: They will be soon, I hope.

DE TORCY: Does this mean a major change in policy?

BOLINGBROKE: That will depend.

DE TORCY: On Parliament or the cabinet?

BOLINGBROKE: On a very frail alliance.

(Meanwhile a card table has been set up at center with an armchair and two straight chairs.)

DUCHESS: Who will be Your Majesty's partners?

QUEEN: You choose.

DUCHESS: Lady Abercrombie?

QUEEN: *(Indicating a lady nearby.)* No, Lady Albemarle.

LADY ALBEMARLE: I thank Your Majesty.

DUCHESS: And for the third player?

QUEEN: The third…my lord ambassador.

(Astonishment in the crowd. Bolingbroke is delighted.)

DUCHESS: *(Reproachfully to the queen.)* Showing such preference…!

QUEEN: What does it matter?

DUCHESS: You see the reaction.

QUEEN: Then you should have chosen someone yourself.

(The Marquis de Torcy has given his hat and gloves to a member of his suite. He offers his hand to the Queen and escorts her to the table, where he sits between her and Lady Albemarle. The Duchess never takes her eyes from them as she crosses left.)

BOLINGBROKE: You are too generous, Your Grace. The *marquis* invited to be the queen's partner! It's more than I asked.

DUCHESS: It's more than I intended.

BOLINGBROKE: The ambassador is not a man to miss an opportunity. See what a friendly chat he's having with Her Majesty.

(And the Duchess starts toward them.)

I wouldn't interrupt if I were you. Watch and listen…because now I think is the moment.

QUEEN: *(Playing a card and seeming to reply to de Torcy.)* You're right, my lord, it is warm in here…stifling… *(Turning to Masham.)* Captain Masham…

(Masham steps forward and bows.)

May I have a glass of water?

DUCHESS: *(Uttering a low cry and starting forward.)* Oh hell!!!

QUEEN: What is wrong with you, duchess?

DUCHESS: *(Struggling to control her rage.)* I…I… Nothing! Your Majesty may possibly…

QUEEN: *(Still seated.)* May what? What do you mean by this outburst?

DUCHESS: Your Majesty may have forgotten…

BOLINGBROKE AND DE TORCY: *(Trying to calm her.)* Your Grace! Madame!

LADY ALBEMARLE: Show some respect for the queen!

QUEEN: *(On her dignity.)* What? What have I forgotten?

DUCHESS: *(Trying to recover.)* The protocol…the prerogatives of etiquette in the palace. It is only proper for one of your ladies in waiting to bring Your Majesty…

QUEEN: *(Surprised.)* All this fuss over that? *(Turning back to the card game.)* Well then, duchess, bring it yourself.

DUCHESS: *(Thunderstruck.)* Me!

(Masham offers the tray and glass of water to her.)

BOLINGBROKE: I must say, Your Grace, that seeing you fetch it yourself…here before the court…is rather enchanting.

(The Duchess can scarcely contain herself as she takes the tray from Masham.)

DUCHESS: Ah!

QUEEN: *(Impatiently.)* Well, Your Grace? Did you hear me? After all your insistence on the privilege…!

(The Duchess, trembling with rage, proffers the glass of water, which spills on the Queen's gown.)

Act IV

QUEEN: *(Rising abruptly.)* Ah! You clumsy cow!

(All rise and Abigail comes down to the Queen.)

DUCHESS: Your Majesty has never spoken to me like that before!

QUEEN: *(Sharply.)* Perhaps I've been too indulgent.

DUCHESS: After all the services I have rendered…

QUEEN: …which I am tired of hearing about.

DUCHESS: If they are unwelcome, I offer Your Majesty my resignation.

QUEEN: I accept. I won't keep you, my lords and ladies; you may retire.

BOLINGBROKE: *(To the duchess.)* You'll have to apologize.

DUCHESS: Never! And that rendezvous will never take place. *(To the Queen.)* One word, ma'am! In resigning my position, I owe Your Majesty an account of the last duty with which I was charged.

BOLINGBROKE: What are you up to?

DUCHESS: On the complaint of Lord Bolingbroke, Your Majesty ordered me to discover the assailant of the late Richard Bolingbroke.

BOLINGBROKE: Oh Lord!

DUCHESS: *(To Bolingbroke.)* You must answer for the culprit now. I turn him over to you. Arrest Captain Masham. There is the guilty man.

QUEEN: *(Stricken.)* Masham! Can it be true?

MASHAM: *(Bowing his head.)* Yes, ma'am.

DUCHESS: *(Softly to Bolingbroke while looking at the queen.)* I am avenged!

BOLINGBROKE: *(Softly to her, grinning.)* But we win!

DUCHESS: *(Fiercely.)* Not yet!

(On a signal from the Queen, Bolingbroke takes Masham's sword. The Queen, supported by Abigail, retires to her apartments. The Duchess goes out rear.)

END OF ACT FOUR

ACT V

Scene: The queen's boudoir. Two doors at the rear. At left French doors opening on a balcony. At right a door to other rooms of the queen's apartments. At left a table and a sofa.

At Rise: Bolingbroke enters at the rear left, Thompson showing him in.

BOLINGBROKE: Thank you, Thompson.

(Thompson withdraws. Abigail enters at rear right.)

ABIGAIL: Ah! You're here already, my lord.

BOLINGBROKE: All doors open wide to me now! Has Her Majesty joined our little alliance? If so, I must give some thought to my cabinet.

ABIGAIL: Cabinet?

BOLINGBROKE: Yes. My appointment as prime minister can't be far off now.

ABIGAIL: It's very far off, I'm afraid.

BOLINGBROKE: What are you telling me?

ABIGAIL: While I was talking with the queen about Arthur... *(On an abrupt tangent.)* He's not in danger, is he?

BOLINGBROKE: None at all. He's paroled to my custody—snugly holed up in the best room of my house. You were saying you and the queen...

ABIGAIL: We were talking, and people began to arrive. First, Lady… Lady—some great lady who is devoted to the duchess.

BOLINGBROKE: Lady Abercrombie?

ABIGAIL: That's the one…with Lord Devonshire and Mister Walpole.

BOLINGBROKE: Friends of the duchess.

ABIGAIL: They came on their own, they said…

BOLINGBROKE: She sent them.

ABIGAIL: …to tell the queen that dismissing the duchess would be disastrous…that the Whig party was furious…and would reject the bill recalling her brother James.

BOLINGBROKE: What did the queen say?

ABIGAIL: Not a word. She seemed unsure of herself, looking around for advice…even to me.

BOLINGBROKE: You should have told her.

ABIGAIL: What do I know about these things?

BOLINGBROKE: What does the Queen's Council know? So…what happened?

ABIGAIL: The queen was still hesitating when Lady Abercrombie began talking to her very quietly…

BOLINGBROKE: About what?

ABIGAIL: I couldn't hear—only a name, Lord Evandale…and Masham!

That I'm sure of. The queen had been looking very cold, but suddenly she smiled and said, "Let her come and I shall see her."

BOLINGBROKE: The duchess—back in the palace? I thought she was gone for good.

ABIGAIL: I didn't know what to do, so I sent for you.

BOLINGBROKE: Was anything agreed upon?

ABIGAIL: About reconciliation?

BOLINGBROKE: *(Impatiently.)* Yes!

ABIGAIL: It was agreed the duchess will come back to return her keys to the queen's private chambers. *(Pointing to the door right.)* Those keys give her access to the queen without being seen.

BOLINGBROKE: Yes, I know.

ABIGAIL: The queen will refuse to take back the keys. The duchess will then fall to her knees; Her Majesty will raise her up and they'll embrace, and the bill will pass, and the Marquis de Torcy will be sent back to Paris.

BOLINGBROKE: Oh weak woman! Weak queen! At the very moment we held victory!

ABIGAIL: It's gone now.

BOLINGBROKE: No, no, Fortune and I know each other too well to part company over this. We've bickered and Fortune has left me sometimes…but she always comes back! Tell me—this reconciliation, this meeting between the queen and the duchess, when is it to be?

ABIGAIL: In half an hour.

BOLINGBROKE: I must speak to Her Majesty.

ABIGAIL: She's with her ministers. That's why I was sent out.

BOLINGBROKE: *(Striking his forehead.)* My God! My God! What do I do now?

ABIGAIL: *(Pointing to door opening up left.)* Sh! The queen…

BOLINGBROKE: *(Quietly.)* Go watch for the duchess and warn me when she comes.

(Abigail curtsies to the Queen and leaves up right.)

QUEEN: *(Brightening as she sees Bolingbroke.)* Ah, it's you, Lord Henry. I'm glad to see you. I have just spent the most trying day!

BOLINGBROKE: *(Smiling and ironic.)* I've heard about Your Majesty's latest clemency to the duchess. It's generous of you to forget yesterday's scandal so quickly.

QUEEN: Forget it? I wish to heaven I could! I've had to listen till my nerves were shrieking about a silly glass of water!

BOLINGBROKE: So you're reconciling with the duchess.

QUEEN: Yes…let's get it over with. Since you want peace too, you'll not be surprised at the sacrifices I have made to obtain it. And then the poor duchess…

(As Bolingbroke shows his astonishment.)

Oh, I'm not defending her! Heaven forbid! But sometimes people accuse her unjustly. Even you. *(Gravely.)* What you told me about her and Captain Masham, for instance. *(Smiling serenely.)* A complete error! It's another man entirely.

BOLINGBROKE: You believe that?

QUEEN: *(Smiling.)* They showed me absolute proof…which I must not mention. *(Confidentially.)* The duchess is very intimate with Lord Evandale.

BOLINGBROKE: *(Summoning a smile.)* Your Majesty calls that proof?

QUEEN: *(Sternly.)* Certainly. There are letters that prove it beyond all doubt. *(Laughing.)* And think about it—I don't know why it never occurred to me—if she loved Masham, would she have denounced him before the whole court yesterday and insisted you arrest him?

BOLINGBROKE: *(Quietly.)* Couldn't it have been jealousy?

QUEEN: What do you imply?

BOLINGBROKE: *(Laughing.)* The duchess suspected…or guessed…that last night Masham had a mysterious interview…

QUEEN: Oh heavens!

BOLINGBROKE: …with whom we do not know. It may not even be true. But if Your Majesty desires, I could find out.

QUEEN: *(Quickly.)* No, no. There's no need.

BOLINGBROKE: What's certain is that after Your Majesty's soirée, the duchess was expecting a rendezvous in her rooms with Masham.

QUEEN: A rendezvous?

BOLINGBROKE: Yes, ma'am.

QUEEN: *(Angrily.)* Last night? With Masham! They had an…an understanding? They were…?

BOLINGBROKE: *(Following up his advantage.)* And imagine her despair today at losing her supervision of you and your affairs! She is deprived of her access to the palace at all hours. She can no longer get at Masham, who is my prisoner. She can no longer see him here, right under your nose, without danger or suspicion. That's why she wants this reconciliation. That's why once she is back here at court…

QUEEN: Never!

(Abigail runs in up right.)

ABIGAIL: *(Anxiously.)* My lord! My lord!

QUEEN: *(Angrily.)* What is it?

ABIGAIL: The duchess! Her carriage is coming into the courtyard.

QUEEN: The duchess! *(Coming center.)* I can pardon personal injuries but never insults to the crown. And yesterday the duchess deliberately insulted her sovereign.

BOLINGBROKE: Publicly.

(Thompson appears at the rear.)

THOMPSON: Her Grace the Duchess of Marlborough attends the orders of Her Majesty.

QUEEN: Abigail, go tell her we cannot see her. We have disposed of the place she occupied in our household. Tomorrow she must return the keys to our apartments, which are henceforth forbidden to her, as is our presence. Go tell her.

ABIGAIL: *(Stupefied.)* Is it possible?

BOLINGBROKE: *(Coolly.)* Go, Miss Abigail. Obey the queen.

ABIGAIL: Yes, my lord. *(Softly to Bolingbroke.)* You are a wizard.

(She leaves up left. Bolingbroke goes to the Queen, who has flung herself down in the armchair at right.)

BOLINGBROKE: Well done, my sovereign, very well done!

QUEEN: *(Flushed with pride.)* It was, wasn't it? They think I'm weak and I'm not.

BOLINGBROKE: I can see that! Speak! We are ready to carry out your orders.

QUEEN: *(Rising.)* My orders? Yes... I'll give them to you as soon as I think of some. Lord Henry, tell me...about Masham...

BOLINGBROKE: He is still my prisoner. We'll deal with him after the new cabinet is formed and the Duke of Marlborough recalled.

QUEEN: Good. I'm going to court–martial him!

BOLINGBROKE: The duke?

QUEEN: No! Masham!

BOLINGBROKE: Oh. Masham.

QUEEN: And I want him punished! Convicted! I want it!

BOLINGBROKE: Oh, Majesty…

QUEEN: He killed your cousin! Besides, the duchess will be furious.

BOLINGBROKE: On the contrary, she'll be delighted. They've quarreled, and it's war to the death between them now.

QUEEN: *(Sweetly, her anger evaporating.)* Oh. You didn't tell me that.

BOLINGBROKE: *(Chuckling.)* She discovered that Masham didn't love her. He never had. He loves someone else.

QUEEN: Are you sure? Who told you?

BOLINGBROKE: He did. My prisoner confessed there's someone at court he adores in secret, although he's never told her. That's all I could get out of him.

QUEEN: *(Contentedly.)* That's different. I mean, that's very strange. But shouldn't we question Masham?

BOLINGBROKE: Yes, we really should. Provided it's in secret and no one suspects.

QUEEN: Why?

BOLINGBROKE: Because I am responsible for him. I must not allow him to communicate with anyone, especially anyone at court. But this evening, when everyone has gone to bed, when there's no danger of being seen…

QUEEN: Yes! That will be best!

(Bolingbroke goes up to the door at the rear.)

BOLINGBROKE: I'll bring my prisoner so that we can interrogate

him…or rather Your Majesty can interrogate him, because I will
not have time…

QUEEN: *(Contentedly.)* Good…good…

(The Duchess opens the door at right for an instant.)

DUCHESS: Oh hell! Bolingbroke!

(She quickly closes the door. The Queen turns at the sound.)

QUEEN: Hush!

BOLINGBROKE: What is it?

QUEEN: *(Nodding right.)* I thought I heard something there. No…
(Coming to him, playfully.) Till this evening…*à bientôt!*

BOLINGBROKE: Masham will be here…before eleven.

*(Bolingbroke goes out up left. The Queen sees him out and turns as
Abigail enters up right. The Queen sits on the sofa left.)*

QUEEN: Ah, there you are, little one. Come sit here by me. Well, what
did the duchess say?

ABIGAIL: Nothing. She just looked daggers.

QUEEN: *(Smiling.)* I can easily believe it. Your message showed her
clearly who her replacement is.

ABIGAIL: *(Surprised.)* What do you mean?

QUEEN: You, Abigail! You are going to be everything for me—my con-
fidante, my friend. That's the way it's going to be. Because today

I reign, I command! Finish your story. You think the duchess is furious?

ABIGAIL: I'm sure of it. Going down the grand staircase she said to the Marchioness of Milford-Haven—Miss Price heard them, and you can believe Miss Price—the duchess said, "If I go under, I'll take the queen with me. I shall disgrace her."

QUEEN: Heavens!

ABIGAIL: And she added, "I have information I can use against her." But then they walked out of earshot and Miss Price couldn't catch any more.

QUEEN: What information was she talking about? Did she mean the interview with Captain Masham we had planned for last night?

ABIGAIL: But you didn't see him! *(With satisfaction.)* And now he's a prisoner, it's impossible.

QUEEN: *(Constrained.)* But…if it were possible?

ABIGAIL: *(Alarmed.)* What do you mean?

QUEEN: *(Unable to contain her joy.)* Abigail! He's coming! I'm expecting him this evening!

ABIGAIL: *(Startled.)* You are, ma'am?

QUEEN: *(Taking her hand.)* What's wrong?

ABIGAIL: I'm afraid…I'm so afraid…

QUEEN: *(Gratefully, rising.)* For me? Don't worry. I'm in no danger.

ABIGAIL: But if the duchess learns he's here…in your apartments! At night! No, Masham is under guard. Lord Henry would never let him go free. It's impossible.

(The Queen indicates the door up left, which is opening and admitting Masham.)

QUEEN: Hush! Here he is.

ABIGAIL: *(Starting toward him.)* Oh heavens!

QUEEN: Don't leave us.

ABIGAIL: *(Jealously.)* No indeed, ma'am. Certainly not.

(Masham advances slowly and bows to the Queen, who beckons him to her with silent emotion.)

QUEEN: *(To Abigail.)* Lock the doors…and come back.

(Abigail locks the doors right and upstage and returns quickly to her place by the Queen.)

MASHAM: Lord Bolingbroke sent me with these papers for Your Majesty. He said he could entrust them to no one but me.

QUEEN: *(Taking the papers with a sweet smile.)* Good. Thank you.

MASHAM: I must bring them back with Your Majesty's signature.

QUEEN: That's true. I was forgetting. *(Sitting at the desk left, looking at the papers.)* Good heavens, how many there are!

(She removes her gloves, takes a pen and quickly signs the various documents without bothering to read them. Meanwhile Masham is with Abigail at the other side of the stage, extreme right.)

ABIGAIL: *(Low and vibrant.)* Listen to me, Arthur. I have the duchess's place now—the same power, the same privileges, the favor of the queen...

MASHAM: Really?

ABIGAIL: And I have decided to give them all up.

MASHAM: Why?

ABIGAIL: For you. Would you do as much for me?

MASHAM: Can you ask me that?

ABIGAIL: Then listen, Arthur. You are loved by a...a very great lady... the first lady of the kingdom.

MASHAM: What are you saying?

ABIGAIL: Sh! *(Motioning toward the approaching queen.)* The queen...

QUEEN: Here you are, Captain—the papers you brought for our signature.

MASHAM: I thank Your Majesty. I'll go now and tell Lord Henry he is prime minister.

QUEEN: That's very generous of you, knowing the first use he makes of his power may be to prosecute the assailant of his cousin Richard Bolingbroke.

MASHAM: I have no fear of that. He knows how the duel happened.

QUEEN: And of course you have friends in high places. You have powerful protectors.

Act V

MASHAM: Ma'am?

QUEEN: Ourself, first of all…and even more powerful—the duchess.

(She sits on the sofa at left. Masham stands before her, and Abigail stands behind the sofa, leaning on the back and watching Masham.)

They assure me you will not confess it, Captain, because you are discreet—but they say you love her.

MASHAM: Oh no, ma'am! Never!

QUEEN: Why deny it? The duchess is very charming, and the rank she holds…

MASHAM: What do rank and power matter when one is in love? *(Looking at Abigail behind the queen.)* And I am in love already.

QUEEN: *(Lowering her gaze.)* Ah! That's different. And is the one you love very beautiful?

MASHAM: More beautiful than I can tell you. Punish me, ma'am, if I dare say it here…

(Noises off.)

QUEEN: *(Jumping to her feet.)* Hush! Do you hear that?

ABIGAIL: *(Indicating the door right.)* They're pounding at the door there.

MASHAM: *(Looking upstage.)* There too.

ABIGAIL: That noise…! There's a crowd outside.

QUEEN: *(To Masham.)* How do you get out now? *(To Abigail.)* If they see him here…!

ABIGAIL: There, on the balcony…

(Masham dashes to the balcony, and Abigail closes the French doors behind him.)

QUEEN: Good… Now open up for them.

ABIGAIL: Yes, ma'am. Calm now, very calm.

QUEEN: Oh, this will be the death of me…

(Abigail unlocks the doors at the rear. The Duchess bursts in and then several Lords, Bolingbroke among them. Abigail unlocks the door right and admits several Maids of Honor.)

Who dares at this hour…in my private apartments! Heavens! The duchess! An outrage like this…!

DUCHESS: *(Scanning the room.)* Your Majesty will forgive the intrusion. It's a matter of national security. There are rumors circulating in the city… *(Focusing on the balcony.)* Lord Marlborough advises me that the French army has attacked at Denain and won a total victory.

BOLINGBROKE: *(Coolly.)* It's true.

(The Duchess makes a dash for the balcony and Abigail steps between her and the Queen.)

DUCHESS: Listen! Do you hear the shouts of the people?

BOLINGBROKE: Demanding peace.

Act V

(The Duchess opens the French doors and cries:)

DUCHESS: Aha! Captain Masham! In the queen's apartments!

QUEEN: I'm lost!

ABIGAIL: Not yet. *(Falling to her knees.)* Mercy, ma'am! Pardon me for not telling you. He came to see me tonight.

DUCHESS: You have the audacity to tell us…!

ABIGAIL: …the truth!

MASHAM: *(Kneeling.)* Let Your Majesty punish us both.

QUEEN: *(Low.)* Lord Henry…!

BOLINGBROKE: *(Addressing the crowd.)* If Your Majesty will permit, I must explain to you…

DUCHESS: …and to me! I demand to know why a prisoner in your charge is free. What reason can there be?

BOLINGBROKE: *(To the assembly.)* A reason to which you would have yielded as I did, all of you. Captain Masham asked me, on his word of honor as a gentleman, for permission to say farewell to Abigail Churchill, his wife!

QUEEN: Oh heavens!

DUCHESS: Oh hell!

QUEEN: *(Signaling the crowd to step back.)* My good people, a moment, I beg of you! *(Coming downstage center with Bolingbroke.)* What have you done?

BOLINGBROKE: *(Low.)* You asked me to save you. Come, come, my queen! It wouldn't do, would it, to disgrace this young girl who sacrifices herself in order to shield Your Majesty?

(The Queen takes it like a queen.)

QUEEN: No. Tell them to approach.

(Bolingbroke signals and Abigail and Masham come forward.)

Abigail, it must be as Lord Bolingbroke has said. Please do not say no. Let this be another proof of your devotion…and my gratitude and friendship are yours forever.

ABIGAIL: *(Effusively.)* Oh, ma'am, if you only knew how hap…

BOLINGBROKE: *(Sternly cutting her off.)* Silence!

(He signals Masham, who in turn approaches the Queen.)

QUEEN: As for you, Captain Masham, I know you may have other desires perhaps…but as a token of the devotion you bear your queen, she asks this of you…

MASHAM: Ma'am?

QUEEN: Your marriage to Abigail—it is our royal will.

(Abigail and Masham bow and retire right. The Queen moves center and addresses the court.)

My lords and ladies, we are recalling His Grace the Duke of Marlborough, whose services are no longer required; and having decided upon an honorable peace, we purpose to open negotiations without delay between our plenipotentiaries and those of France.

Act V

(Bolingbroke is at right between Abigail and Masham.)

BOLINGBROKE: *(Confidentially.)* You see, Abigail, this bears out my theory: Marlborough overthrown…Europe at peace…

MASHAM: *(Giving him the papers the queen has signed.)* …Bolingbroke prime minister…

BOLINGBROKE: …all thanks to a glass of water!

END OF PLAY

BIOGRAPHY

ROBERT CORNTHWAITE was born in St. Helens, Oregon, went through grammar and high school in Portland, and completed his formal education at the University of Southern California. By that time a war had intervened and the U.S. and Royal Air Forces had escorted him around the Mediterranean for three fascinating years.

After the war he went back into radio. Films followed in 1950. That year he appeared in six features, including a lead in Howard Hawks' *The Thing.* Nineteen-fifty was also the year he became a Blackfoot Indian. He was adopted into the tribe by Chief Joe Iron Pipe, dressed in feathers and speaking Sioux, all for the greater glory of RKO. More than sixty feature films have ensued and hundreds of play productions and even more episodes of television, perhaps most memorably as the demented mayor on *Picket Fences* who died nude on a rocking horse.

Mr. Cornthwaite's translations of Pirandello have played at the Arena Stage, Washington, D.C.; Oregon Shakespeare Festival, Ashland and Portland; Seattle Repertory; East West Players, Los Angeles; San José; Niagara-on-the-Lake; and several other regional theaters around the U.S. and Canada as well as the Roundabout in New York.